Children's Books on Ancient Greek and Roman Mythology

Recent Titles in
Bibliographies and Indexes in World Literature

Vanguardism in Latin American Literature: An Annotated Bibliographical Guide
Merlin H. Forster and K. David Jackson, compilers

Donald Davie: A Checklist of His Writings, 1946-1988
Stuart Wright, compiler

Recent Studies in Myths and Literature, 1970-1990: An Annotated Bibliography
Bernard Accardi, David J. Charlson, Frank A. Doden, Richard F. Hardin,
Sung Ryol Kim, Sonya J. Lancaster, and Michael H. Shaw, compilers

Robinson Crusoe: A Bibliographical Checklist of English Language Editions
(1719-1979)
Robert W. Lovett, assisted by Charles C. Lovett

The Soviet Union in Literature for Children and Young Adults: An Annotated
Bibliography of English-Language Books
Frances F. Povsic, compiler

The Indian Subcontinent in Literature for Children and Young Adults: An
Annotated Bibliography of English-Language Books
Meena Khorana, compiler

Contemporary Spanish American Poets: A Bibliography of Primary and
Secondary Sources
Jacobo Sefamí, compiler

British Science Fiction: A Chronology, 1478-1990
Nicholas Ruddick

The Latin American Short Story: An Annotated Guide to Anthologies and
Criticism
Daniel Balderston, compiler

Caribbean Women Novelists: An Annotated Critical Bibliography
Lizabeth Paravisini-Gebert and Olga Torres-Seda, compilers

Clockworks: A Multimedia Bibliography of Works Useful for the Study of
the Human/Machine Interface in SF
Richard D. Erlich and Thomas P. Dunn, compilers

Oscar Wilde: An Annotated Bibliography
Thomas A. Mikolyzk, compiler

Modern Verse Drama in English: An Annotated Bibliography
Kayla McKinney Wiggins, compiler

Children's Books on Ancient Greek and Roman Mythology

An Annotated Bibliography

Compiled by
Antoinette Brazouski and Mary J. Klatt

Bibliographies and Indexes in World Literature, Number 40

Greenwood Press
Westport, Connecticut • London

Library of Congress Cataloging-in-Publication Data

Brazouski, Antoinette.
    Children's books on ancient Greek and Roman mythology : an
annotated bibliography / compiled by Antoinette Brazouski and Mary
J. Klatt.
        p.   cm.—(Bibliographies and indexes in world literature,
    ISSN 0742-6801 ; no. 40)
    Includes index.
    ISBN 0-313-28973-5 (alk. paper)
    1. Mythology, Classical—Juvenile literature—Abstracts.
    2. Mythology, Classical—Juvenile literature—Bibliography.
    I. Klatt, Mary J. II. Title. III. Series.
    BL722.B72   1994
    292.1'3—dc20   93-29896

British Library Cataloguing in Publication Data is available.

Library of Congress Catalog Card Number: 93-29896
ISBN: 0-313-28973-5
ISSN: 0742-6801

First published in 1994

Greenwood Press, 88 Post Road West, Westport, CT 06881
An imprint of Greenwood Publishing Group, Inc.

Printed in the United States of America

The paper used in this book complies with the
Permanent Paper Standard issued by the National
Information Standards Organization (Z39.48-1984).

10 9 8 7 6 5 4 3 2 1

Contents

Preface

The study of ancient Greek and Roman mythology has been recognized as an important part of the education of children because it stimulates imagination, which is an essential element of any creative endeavor. In *Children and Their Literature*, Constantine Georgiou notes that nature myths are especially appealing to the young child's curiosity about the causes of natural phenomena, that the myths about heroes who successfully face many challenges supply models for middle-school children in their struggle to grow up, and that myths with deep symbolic significance give adolescents an understanding of how the actions of one individual influence the lives of many others (p. 230). Finally, myths entertain and provide a brief escape from reality.

Because of its interrelationships with many other disciplines, the study of ancient Greek and Roman mythology has various applications in the elementary school classroom--most often as a part of literary studies. It goes without saying that in Western literature there are numerous allusions to ancient Greek and Roman myths. Early exposure to the myths not only frees one from the necessity of consulting footnotes and/or reference books but, more important, as Ted Hughes has pointed out, enables a single name or word to evoke a wealth of enriching associations. William F. Russell maintains that myths allow one access to the shared knowledge of one's culture and serve as mental "hooks" for gathering and collecting new ideas (p. 2). To the objection that study of the traditional is elitist or limiting, Marcia Muelder Eaton answers that communication and alteration of attitudes are made possible by shared traditions, which are not static and constrictive but rather fluid and open, providing a link between the past and the future (p. 101). Although Eaton is speaking about art, her comments apply equally well to literature. Influenced by the work of Jean Piaget, William Anderson and Patrick Groff observe that the thinking of children under eleven strongly tends toward mythic representation rather than abstraction of concepts (p. 53). As a result, the child is naturally drawn to mythic literature.

Since they contain folktale motifs, literary archetypes, and universal themes, ancient Greek and Roman myths can be used either to introduce or in connection with the literature of other nations. The ancient myths reveal the chronological as well as the geographical universality of the human experience. As Michelle P. and Robert M. Wilhelm point out, myths provide the student with a means of affirming his or her humanity and of determining his or her place in the world (p. 14). Charlotte Huck (pp. 703-704) states that the theme of the hero's journey and return home, which is symbolic of the individual's journey through life (cf. Joseph Campbell, *The Hero With A Thousand Faces*, especially p. 36), is found not only in ancient Greek mythological works such as Homer's *Odyssey* but also in modern children's books, including *Sounder* by William H. Armstrong, *Julia of the Wolves* by Jean George, *Call It Courage* by Armstrong Sperry, *A Wrinkle in Time* by Madeleine L'Engle, and *Where the Wild Things Are* by Maurice Sendak. Mary Ann Paulin (p. 209) notes that the Pygmalion motif occurs in Algernon D. Black's *The Woman of the Wood: A Tale from Old Russia*. The folktale motif of the jealous sisters/stepsisters, associated with the story of Cinderella, is found in the myth of Psyche.

In literature classes ancient Greek and Roman myths can serve as the basis of various literary activities. In *Literature and the Child*, Bernice E. Cullinan et al. suggest ways in which the myths may be used to explore literary concepts, such as theme, plot structure, mood, and character development (pp. 188-195). In an article in *Elementary English*, Arlene M. Pillar presents lesson plans for integrating ancient Greek mythology into a literature program (pp. 428-431). Because of its broad scope, ancient Greek and Roman mythology is ideal for familiarizing children with various types of stories including creation myths, etiological myths (*Just So* stories), adventure tales, and love stories. It can also be employed to introduce more advanced students to the major literary genres, particularly epic poetry. In *Children and Books*, May Hill Arbuthnot and Zena Sutherland emphasize that the amount of classroom time needed to develop proper appreciation of ancient Greek and Roman epics is time well spent (p. 200). Jayne Ilene Hanlin finds that the epics serve as an excellent basis for writing assignments and that by comparing different variants of the same myth, students gain insights into the manner in which an author creates his or her own unique version of a story (p. 56). Writing assignments and other activities for secondary level students which can be "downsized" for elementary schoolers are found at the end of each chapter of Hugh Hollinghurst's *Gods and Heroes of Ancient Greece*. Northrop Frye states that by reading myths simply as stories rather than as repositories of hidden meanings, the student begins to comprehend the difference between imaginative and discursive writing (p. 116). On the other hand, reading different interpretations of the same myth makes clear the difference between the literal meaning and the allegorical meaning of a story. John Warren Stewig advocates the dramatization of myths to teach children how to interpret and improvise (pp. 199-200). Finally, as Isaac Asimov's *Words from the Myths* demonstrates, the study of ancient Greek and Roman mythology contributes to vocabulary development.

The study of the ancient Greek and Roman myths fits into the social studies program as well as into the literature program of the elementary school. Reading a myth (particularly a literal translation of an ancient work of literature) allows the student to come into contact with an actual product of an ancient mind. Whenever scenes from daily life are included in a myth, history comes alive; and much cultural, not to mention archaeological, information is absorbed almost without effort. Myths frequently explain the origins of social institutions. They feature objects, such as the toga, and attitudes, such as the need for hospitality, that are associated with ancient Greece and/or Rome. Even the activities of the deities, who are anthropomorphic, are reflections of human activities. Many ancient Roman myths, since they are adaptations of Greek myths, are set in Greece and mirror Greek culture as well as Roman. Some classical myths contain references to other ancient cultures. Midas, king of Phrygia, wears a *tiara* (an Asiatic turban) to cover his ass' ears. Dionysus has the elaborate clothing and perfumed hair associated with Eastern monarchs. Memnon leads a contingent of Ethiopians to Troy. Noting cultural similarities and differences arouses interest in the study of still other cultures and their mythologies.

Requiring students to read stories about mythological heroes as well as historical ones has long been considered a good method of introducing children to the study of history (see History of Children's Books on Greek and Roman Mythology in the United States, p. 5). Such reading not only reveals the personal qualities of heroes such as courage, perseverance, and loyalty to country and fellow combatants but also offers role models for emulation. Furthermore, as Edgar Jones has demonstrated, in ancient hero myths, human aggression is channeled into good action, namely, the fight against evil, which, he says, is generally personified as a monster (p. 32).

One of the objectives of both literary and historical studies is to foster the psychological and moral development of the child. The ancient Greek and Roman myths are suited to this function, especially in a secular, religiously neutral school system. Stewig points out that many myths, like that of King Midas, were prescriptive of desirable behavior which is still desirable today (p. 185). Edna Johnson et al. say that a theme underlying all ancient Greek myths is the obligation of the human being to maintain the basic nobility of his or her nature in all circumstances (p. 388). David L. Russell states that myths tend to lessen fear of the unknown, especially of death. He goes on to say that since it is the most humanistic of all world mythologies, ancient Greek and Roman mythology offers the best insights into human nature and the problems which stem from man's relationship with the supernatural, with family members, friends, lovers, and enemies (pp. 59-60). Johnson et al. believe that the study of ancient Greek mythology develops in the child not only an awareness of order, proportion, and harmony but also an appreciation of nature, of the wonder of man, and of life in general (p. 388).

Elizabeth Cook finds that using ancient Greek and Roman myths with a class composed of culturally and/or economically diverse students fosters corporate unity among the students while freeing them from the effects of social prejudices mirrored in contemporary realistic literature (p. 8). Since the mythological characters are both fictional and removed in time and circumstance, their actions can be viewed and evaluated objectively; yet, they can be identified with. David L. Russell observes that mythological characters, like young children, perceive themselves as the center of their worlds and that they offer children the hope that like them, the children, through sheer determination, will overcome life's obstacles (p. 61).

The ancient Greek and Roman myths provide a temporary escape from the realities of life. They allow the child to experience emotions with no strings attached. For example, the child can feel terror at Medusa, secure in the knowledge that he or she is perfectly safe. Since ancient authors, particularly Homer, tend to supply only a minimum of descriptive detail, the young reader must use imagination to fill in the picture. The employment of imagination makes the child comfortable in the world of literature, where, as Frye has shown, what one meets--no matter how realistic it seems--is neither real nor unreal (pp. 62-63).

An active imagination is also an asset in the study of the fine arts, another area of scholarship to which ancient Greek and Roman mythology is linked. As a quick perusal of *The Oxford Guide to Classical Mythology in the Arts, 1300-1900s* demonstrates, there are countless paintings and musical compositions that one cannot fully appreciate without knowledge of the mythological personages and incidents featured in them. For example, learning that medieval portraits of the devil were often based on ancient representations of Pan is somehow enlightening. Sandra L. Burwell found that ancient Greek myths could be effectively employed to teach narrative drawing and, at the same time, to arouse interest in ancient Greek art works and techniques, not to mention in the myths themselves. In one of his "How to . . ." books, Arthur Zaidenberg gives children directions for drawing mythical creatures (see Annotated Bibliography). Lorinda Munson Bryant discusses several famous works of art based on classical myths in *The Children's Book of Celebrated Legends* (see Annotated Bibliography).

In the physical sciences, too, acquaintance with mythological characters and their stories widens the child's perspective by revealing the origins of scientific terms, such as *Achilles' tendon* and *arachnophobia*. Moreover, it makes clear how myth can serve as primitive science; for example, the thunderbolt was thought to be the weapon of Zeus. Creation myths are clearly an attempt to explain the origin of the universe.

Last but not least, the study of ancient Greek and Roman mythology heightens awareness of the mythological symbols encountered in daily life, such as the *caduceus*, the messenger's staff of Hermes (the familiar figure on the logo of the FTD Florists), which serves as the symbol of the United States Medical Corps.

The purpose of this book is to facilitate the selection of elementary-school-level books on ancient Greek and Roman mythology. With the exception of *The Story of the Iliad* by F. S. Marvin, all the books listed in the Annotated Bibliography were available through interlibrary loan as of January 1, 1993, the cut-off date of the bibliography. Each book has been reviewed with critical rather than descriptive annotations. Because readers' tastes and purposes vary, the reviews have been kept as objective as possible; however, particular attention has been paid to how faithfully the reteller of the myth followed the ancient accounts. All serious deviations from ancient sources have been noted. In the few reviews where there are no specific comments on the authenticity of the storyline, it may be assumed that the author remained true to the ancient accounts. The degree of proximity to an ancient work is especially important to those who are searching for books to serve as an introduction to literary masterpieces. Moreover, scholars in the area of children's literature, not to mention classicists, tend to think that the best adaptations are those which can be easily comprehended by the child and yet retain both the plot and the tone of the original work (see Constant, pp. 359-362; Arbuthnot and Sutherland, p. 197; Cullinan et al., pp. 189-190; and Huck, p. 219). Still, free retellings can be useful at times. In the reviews, comments about the illustrations in the various books concern their subjects and their relevance to the text. They are not judgments of artistic merit. The grade level suggested for a book refers to the average student of that grade level. Though the reading ability of individuals within a particular grade level varies greatly, it is hoped that the rankings will at least distinguish the easier books from the more difficult ones.

Because they are fables rather than myths, the stories of Aesop have been excluded from the Annotated Bibliography though Marilynne K. Roach's *Two Roman Mice* (see Annotated Bibliography) is ultimately based on one of these stories. Only a few collections--famous and/or easily accessible ones--have been included in the bibliography. Most anthologies contain selections from books listed in the bibliography.

Modern children's books on ancient Greek and Roman mythology retell stories drawn from a variety of ancient works produced during various periods of Greek and Roman history (Fascinated by Greek myths, the Romans adopted and adapted them, often merely changing the names of the deities). Accounts of the creation of the universe are usually based on Hesiod's *Theogony* (Greek, 8th century B.C.). Books on the Trojan War and its aftermath center around events described in three ancient epics: the *Iliad* and *Odyssey* of Homer (Greek, possibly 9th century B.C.) and the *Aeneid* of Vergil (Latin, 1st century B.C.); but writers often add incidents narrated by authors of later antiquity, such as Quintus Smyrnaeus (Greek, probably 4th century A.D.). The Greek tragedians of the fifth century B.C. provide material for accounts of Prometheus

(Aeschyhus), of Oedipus and his family (Sophocles), of Alcestis (Euripides) as well as of various other mythological characters. To present the story of Jason, modern writers frequently combine material from the *Medea* of Euripides and the *Argonautica* of Apollonius Rhodius (Greek, 3rd century B.C.). In creating biographies of heroes, especially Heracles, Theseus, Bellerophontes and Perseus, modern writers often flesh out the accounts of the compiler/summarizer of myths Apollodorus (Greek, earliest possible date middle of the 1st century B.C.). Plutarch's *Theseus* (Greek, 1st century A.D.) supplies further information about that hero. Stories about constellations are derived from Aratus' *Phenomena* (Greek, 3rd century B.C.), from Manilius' *Astronomica* (Latin, 1st century A.D.), or from Hyginus' *Fabulae* (Latin, possibly 2nd century A.D.). The myth of Arion and the dolphins is found in Herodotus' *History* (Greek, 5th century B.C.) while that of Cupid and Psyche comes from the *Metamorphoses*, or *Golden Ass*, of Apuleius (Latin, 2nd century A.D.). Descriptions of some mythical monsters are taken from Pliny the Elder's *Natural History* (Latin, 1st century A.D.). Greek lyric poets, including Simonides (c. 550-c. 468 B.C.), Bacchylides (c. 505-c. 450 B.C.), Pindar (c. 522-c. 442 B.C.), Theocritus (fl. c. 270 B.C.), and Bion (fl. c. 100 B.C.) as well as the *Homeric Hymns* (Greek and of various dates) provide individual mythological incidents, for example, the birth of Iamus (Pindar, *Olympian Odes* 6.27-70). The *Library of History* of Diodorus Siculus (Greek, 1st century B.C.) and the *Description of Greece* of the geographer Pausanias (Greek, 2nd century A.D.) supply numerous local myths, often giving alternative little-known versions of myths. The source of many of the most famous myths, for example, that of King Midas and the golden touch, is the *Metamorphoses* of the Roman poet Ovid, which is a mythological history of the world from the creation of the world to the time of Augustus, during whose prinicipate Ovid (43 B.C.-18 A.D.) was writing. Modern stories about Roman legendary figures like Romulus are generally retellings of accounts of the Roman historian Livy, a contemporary of Ovid.

For more detailed information about the ancient authors and their literary sources, see *The Oxford Companion to Classical Literature*. Those wishing to pinpoint the ancient source of a myth will find *The Meridian Handbook of Classical Mythology*, edited by Edward Tripp, and *The Greek Myths* by Robert Graves especially helpful. An excellent source for Greek and Roman works of literature is the Loeb Classical Library series, which not only gives the Greek or Latin text but also provides a fairly literal translation (pages of text and translation are alternated for easy reference).

The sources of the Annotated Bibliography in this book are multifarious. Several steps were taken to locate the various titles which were to be included in the bibliography. Major reference books were surveyed to identify titles. These included the general works *Children's Books in Print*, *Children's Catalog*, *Children's Books for Schools and Libraries*, and *Cumulative Book Index*. Specialized bibliographies were also consulted: Mary Huse Eastman's *Index to*

Fairy Tales, Myths and Legends; Norma Olin Ireland's *Index to Fairy Tales, Including Folklore, Legends, and Mythology in Collections*; and Rita T. Kohn's *Mythology for Young People: A Reference Guide*. Critical works on children's literature which contain selective bibliographies were surveyed, for example, May Hill Arbuthnot and Zena Sutherland's *Children and Books* and Jan Bingham and Grayce Scholt's *Fifteen Centuries of Children's Literature: An Annotated Chronology of British and American Works in Historical Context*. Titles were also found in references and bibliographies of books and articles dealing with classical mythology, including various children's mythology books. Still other titles were located using the online union catalog of *OCLC Online Computer Library Center, Inc*. An author/title search was performed for each book on the master list. A comprehensive author search was performed for each author in order to determine whether a particular author had written any other books on classical mythology for children that did not appear in the standard reference works or bibliographies. For each major mythological character, a subject search was performed in the *OCLC* union catalog using the *Epic* search service. Key words such as mythology, classical literature, names of heroes, etc. were combined with juvenile literature terms. Finally, a master list of authors and titles was compiled using the aforementioned sources.

An Index to Introductory Material precedes the indices to the Annotated Bibliography. The numbers in this index refer to pages, not annotated entry numbers. The entries in the Annotated Bibliography are arranged alphabetically by author. The indices to the Annotated Bibliography include a title index, an illustrator index, a chronological index, a mythological index, and a general index which includes subject headings, such as "hero myths." The numbers in these indices refer to the entry numbers in the Annotated Bibliography.

We wish to express our gratitude to those who helped make this book possible. Joyce Forney, Interlibrary Loan Assistant at Loyola University of Chicago Medical Center Library, ordered and processed most of the books listed in the bibliography. Without her assistance, the project would have taken much longer to complete. Denise Cronkhite, Night Supervisor at Loyola University of Chicago Medical Center Library, assisted in locating bibliographic records in OCLC. These records contributed to the accuracy of the citations in the bibliography. Jan Behnke and Cathy Melone, both involved in intracampus loans at Loyola University of Chicago Medical Center Library, ordered and processed the materials used in the introductory chapters.

Special thanks is extended to Professor Jack Weiner of Northern Illinois University for recommending Manuscript Services and to Professor D. Raymond Tourville, former acting head of the Department of Foreign Languages and Literatures of Northern Illinois University and Frederic W. Murray, Chairperson of the Department of Foreign Languages and Literatures of Northern Illinois University, for permission to use Manuscript Services.

We owe our most sincere gratitude to the staff of Manuscript Services of Northern Illinois University. Karen M. Blaser, director, coordinated the preparation of the book's manuscript. Last but of critical importance, Jonie Barshinger spent endless hours deciphering minuscule handwriting and patiently inputting the many versions of our text.

References and Uncited Sources

Anderson, William and Groff, Patrick. *A New Look at Children's Literature.* Belmont, California: Wadsworth Publishing Company, Inc., 1972.

Arbuthnot, May Hill and Sutherland, Zena. *Children and Books.* Glenview, Ill.: Scott, Foresman and Company, 1972.

Armstrong, William H. *Sounder.* Illustrated by James Barkley. New York: Harper and Row, 1969.

Asimov, Isaac. *Words from the Myths.* New York: New American Library, 1969.

Bingham, Jan and Scholt, Grayce. *Fifteen Centuries of Children's Literature: An Annotated Chronology of British and American Works in Historical Context.* Westport, Conn.: Greenwood Press, 1980.

Black, Algernon D. *The Woman of the Wood: A Tale from Old Russia.* Illustrated by Evaline Ness. New York: Holt, Rinehart and Winston, 1973.

Burwell, Sandra L. "Greek Myths: A Lesson in Narrative Drawing." *School Arts* 85, no. 1 (September 1985): 22-26.

Campbell, Joseph. *The Hero With a Thousand Faces.* Princeton, New Jersey: Princeton University Press, 1968.

Children's Books for Schools and Libraries. New York: R. R. Bowker Co., 1961-.

Children's Books in Print. New York: R. R. Bowker Company, 1983-.

Children's Catalog. New York: H. W. Wilson, 1916-.

Constant, Helen. *A Critical Study of Selected Greek Myths as Story for Children.* Thesis, Columbia University. Ann Arbor, Mich.: University Microfilms, 1970.

Cook, Elizabeth. *The Ordinary and the Fabulous: An Introduction to Myths, Legends, and Fairy Tales.* Cambridge: Cambridge University Press, 1976.

Cullinan, Bernice E.; Karrer, Mary K.; and Pillar, Arlene M. *Literature and the Child.* New York: Harcourt Brace Jovanovich, Inc., 1981.

Cumulative Book Index. New York: H. W. Wilson, 1904-.

Eastman, Mary Huse. *Index to Fairy Tales, Myths and Legends.* Boston: Boston Book Company, 1915.

Eastman, Mary Huse. *Index to Fairy Tales, Myths and Legends.* 2d ed. Boston: Boston Book Company, 1926.

Eastman, Mary Huse. *Index to Fairy Tales, Myths and Legends.* Supplement 1. Boston: Boston Book Company, 1937.

Eastman, Mary Huse. *Index to Fairy Tales, Myths and Legends*. Supplement 2. Boston: Boston Book Company, 1952.

Eaton, Marcia Muelder. "Context, Criticism, and Art Education: Putting Meaning into the Life of Sisyphus." *Journal of Aesthetic Education* 24, no. 1 (Spring 1990): 25-34.

Frye, Northrop. *The Educated Imagination*. Bloomington: Indiana University Press, 1964.

George, Jean Craighead. *Julia of the Wolves*. Illustrated by John Schoenherr. New York: Harper and Row, 1972.

Georgiou, Constantine. *Children and Their Literature*. Englewood Cliffs, New Jersey: Prentice Hall, Inc., 1969.

Graves, Michael. *The Greek Myths*. 2 vols. New York: Penguin Books, 1992.

Hanlin, Jayne Ilene. "Give Classics a Front-Row Seat . . ." *Learning* 20, no. 5 (January 1992): 54-57.

Hollinghurst, Hugh. *Gods and Heroes of Ancient Greece*. Illustrated by Raymond Pitt. London: Heinemann Educational Books, 1973.

Howatson, M. C. *The Oxford Companion to Classical Literature*. New York: Oxford University Press, 1989.

Huck, Charlotte S. *Children's Literature in the Elementary School*. 3rd ed., updated. New York: Holt, Rinehart and Winston, 1979.

Hughes, Ted. "Myth and Education: Why was Plato so respectful of the myths and tales which formed the imaginative world of the Greek poets?" *The Times Educational Supplement* (London, September 2, 1977): no page numbers.

Ireland, Norma Olin. *Index to Fairy Tales, Including Folklore, Legends, and Mythology in Collections, 1949-1973*. Supplement 3. Westwood, Mass.: F. W. Faxon Co., 1973.

Ireland, Norma Olin. *Index to Fairy Tales, Including Folklore, Legends, and Mythology in Collections, 1973-1979*. Supplement 4. Westwood, Mass.: F. W. Faxon Co., 1979.

Johnson, Edna; Sickels, Evelyn R.; and Sayers, Frances Clarke. *Anthology of Children's Literature*. 3rd rev. ed. Boston: Houghton Mifflin Company, 1959.

Jones, Edgar. "Ancient Myths and Modern Children." *Use of English* 37, no. 1 (Autumn 1985): 25-34.

Kohn, Rita T. *Mythology for Young People: A Reference Guide*. New York: Garland Publishers, 1985.

L'Engle, Madeleine. *A Wrinkle in Time*. New York: Farrar, Straus & Giroux, 1962.

Paulin, Mary Ann. *Creative Uses of Children's Literature*. Hamden, Conn.: Library Professional Publications, 1982.

Pillar, Arlene M. "Selected Greek Myths: A Critical Appreciation." *Elementary English* 51 (1974): 427-431.

Reid, Jane Davidson. *The Oxford Guide to Classical Mythology in the Arts, 1300-1900s*. New York: Oxford University Press, 1993.

Russell, David L. *Literature for Children: A Short Introduction*. New York: Longman, 1991.

Russell, William F. *Classic Myths to Read Aloud*. New York: Crown Publishers, 1989.

Sendak, Maurice. *Where the Wild Things Are*. Illustrated by Maurice Sendak. New York: Harper and Row, 1963.

Sperry, Armstrong. *Call It Courage*. Illustrated by Armstrong Sperry. New York: Macmillan, 1940.

Stewig, John Warren. *Children and Literature*. Chicago: Rand McNally Publishing Company, 1980.

Tripp, Edward, ed. *The Meridian Handbook of Classical Mythology*. New York: New American Library, 1974.

Ward, Winifred, ed. *Stories to Dramatize*. Anchorage, Kentucky: The Children's Theatre Press, 1952.

White, Mary Lou. *Children's Literature: Criticism and Response*. Columbus, Ohio: Charles E. Merrill Publishing Co., 1976.

Wilhelm, Michelle P. and Wilhelm, Robert M. "Bringing the Classics to Life." *Humanities* 12, no. 1 (January-February 1991): 13-16.

Winkel, Lois. *The Elementary School Library Collection: A Guide to Books and Other Media*. 17th ed. Williamsport, Pennsylvania: Brodart Co., 1990.

Children's Books on Ancient Greek and Roman Mythology

History of Children's Books on Greek and Roman Mythology in the United States

Except for their diction, children's books on ancient Greek and Roman mythology are essentially timeless since they contain traditional material; nevertheless, as Nathaniel Hawthorne pointed out in the preface of *A Wonder Book*, "by their indestructibility itself, they are legitimate subjects for every age to clothe with its own garniture of manners and sentiment, and to imbue with its own morality" (p. 3). A survey of children's books on classical mythology (grammar school level) from Hawthorne's day to the present gives credence to Hawthorne's words by providing insights into the manner in which historical situations, social trends, and attitudes toward education have influenced the retelling of myths. This information, it is hoped, will prove helpful in guiding educators in the selection and understanding of juvenile books on classical mythology.

Hawthorne was the first major American writer to make ancient Greek and Roman myths into literature (as opposed to didactic tracts) for children. In both *A Wonder Book* (1852) and *Tanglewood Tales* (1853), Hawthorne retold the myths freely. He added details; for example, he gave King Midas a daughter who was turned into gold by her father's touch. Hawthorne even altered plot lines. According to Hawthorne, Ariadne tells Theseus that she cannot leave Crete because she must care for her aged father. In the ancient sources, Ariadne sails off with Theseus, who then abandons her. For a thorough analysis of Hawthorne's use of his sources, the most important of which was Charles Anthon's *A Classical Dictionary*, see Hugo McPherson's *Hawthorne as Myth-Maker*, pp. 47-107.

Hawthorne's retellings of myths are reflective of the Romantic Period, the age during which he lived. The tableau with which *A Wonder Book* begins reveals that Hawthorne shared his contemporaries' interest in nature:

Beneath the porch of the country-seat call Tanglewood, one fine autumnal morning, was assembled a merry party of little folks, with a tall youth in the midst of them. They had planned a nutting expedition, and were impatiently waiting for the mists to roll up the hill-slopes, and for the sun to pour the warmth of the Indian Summer over the fields and pastures, and into the nooks of the many-colored woods. There was the prospect of as fine a day as ever gladdened the aspect of this beautiful and comfortable world. As yet, however, the morning mist filled up the whole length and breadth of the valley, above which, on a gently sloping eminence, the mansion stood (p. 5).

Richard D. Hathaway has shown that Hawthorne, like other writers of the Romantic movement, idealized the child (p. 163), taking the child as the symbol of unspoiled innocence (p. 170) and emphasized the parent-child relationship, partly by making use of the then popular theme of separation of mother and child (pp. 168-169). The motif of the brotherhood of man, which McPherson found in nearly all of Hawthorne's mythological tales (*Hawthorne as Myth-Maker*, p. 108), was prominent in the writings of the Transcendentalists, many of whom were involved in abolitionist movements. Nineteenth century customs and attitudes are also revealed in Hawthorne's anachronisms. For example, King Midas wears a suit with pockets and uses spectacles to enhance his vision. He carries a handkerchief hemmed for him by his young daughter.

In *A Wonder Book*, Hawthorne provided a narrator for his stories, a narrator whom he describes as a Yankee (a reminder that this is the pre-Civil-War period in America), a student from Williams College, who is a guest at the summer estate of a Mr. Pringle, who (according to the preface of *Tanglewood Tales*) like his guest, was classically learned. Aristocratic in tone, the preface reflects the fact that during most of the nineteenth century, only upper class boys received a college education, of which Classical Studies was an integral part. Hawthorne's narrator regrets that myths "have not been long ago put into picture-books for little girls and boys. But instead of that, old gray-bearded grandsires pore over them, in misty volumes of Greek and puzzle themselves with trying to find out when, and how, and for what, they were made" (*A Wonder Book*, p. 9). The latter part of the narrator's statement mirrors the interest of the age in the scientific investigation of myths for insights into ancient Greek and Roman culture.

Hawthorne believed that the ancient myths in their original form were unsuitable for children. In the preface to *Tanglewood Tales*, he mused,

These old legends, so brimming over with everything that is most abhorrent to our Christianized moral-sense--some of them so hideous--others so melancholy and miserable, amid which the Greek Tragedians sought their themes, and moulded them into the sternest forms of grief that ever the world saw;--was such material the stuff that children's play-things should be made of! How were they to be purified? How was the blessed sunshine to be thrown into them? (pp. 178-179)

In a letter (dated 1849) to one of the most outstanding educators of the time, Horace Mann, who insisted that reading materials should arouse the child's curiosity, Hawthorne solicited suggestions for the composition of an appropriate work:

. . . I think of writing a schoolbook, or, at any rate, a book for the young,--and should highly prize your advice as to what is wanted, and how it should be achieved (Lathrop, p. 108).

When he wrote his juvenile books, Hawthorne employed several techniques to make the ancient myths suitable for children. He bowdlerized the stories. In the ancient works of literature, Iobates assigns Bellerophontes the task of slaying the Chimaera in the hope that Bellerophontes will be killed. In Hawthorne's "The Chimaera," Iobates proposes the task in order that Bellerophontes may demonstrate his valor and thereby win the admiration of all mankind. In "The Miraculous Pitcher," an unending supply of milk rather than wine comes out of Baucis' pitcher. Hawthorne lightened the tone of the ancient myths; for example, Pandora is a completely carefree child who lives in a paradise rather than a beautiful creature created as a punishment for man. Hawthorne also gave each story as happy an ending as possible. To make the myths more lively, he greatly increased the amount of dialogue and descriptive detail, focusing in on some parts of the myths while summarizing or omitting others. To make the myths more understandable, in *A Wonder Book* through the use of a narrator and in *Tanglewood Tales* by writing as an author/narrator, Hawthorne added both explanatory material and moral commentary. In his retellings, he emphasized that virtue was rewarded, lack of it punished; for example, in "The Miraculous Pitcher," the narrator comments,

The milk-pitcher, I must not forget to say, retained its marvellous quality of being never empty, when it was desirable to have it full. Whenever an honest, good-humored, and free-hearted guest took a draught from this pitcher, he invariably found it the sweetest and most invigorating fluid, that ever ran down his throat. But if a cross and disagreeable curmudgeon happened to sip, he was pretty certain to twist his visage into a hard knot, and pronounce it a pitcher of sour milk (*A Wonder Book*, p. 136).

Hawthorne's concern about morality is representative of the age which saw the development of the Society for Promoting Christian Knowledge, The Church

Missionary Society, the Salvation Army, and the Sunday School Union as well as various temperance and slavery abolitionist groups.

Unlike most of his contemporaries but like Horace Mann, Hawthorne believed that religious teachings in children's literature should be nonsectarian. To rid the myths of pagan elements, Hawthorne changed all of the mythological deities into somewhat mysterious human beings who had the attributes of their divine counterparts; for example, in "The Golden Fleece," Hera is an old lady with a peacock. Toying with the child's willingness to suspend disbelief, Hawthorne used ambiguity to explain away the supernatural or the unbelievable. Describing Jason's reaction to the pronouncement of the Talking Oak, Hawthorne wrote,

> When it [the voice] was quite gone, Jason felt inclined to doubt whether he had actually heard the words, or whether his fancy had not shaped them out of the ordinary sound made by a breeze, while passing through the thick foliage of the tree (p. 341).

The amount of moral and theological material in Hawthorne's works is slight in comparison with that found in *The Heroes; or Greek Fairy Tales for My Children* (1855) by the Anglican cleric Charles Kingsley--a book that attained great popularity in the United States as well as abroad. Addressing his children in his preface, Kingsley says that the true meaning of all the stories which he includes in his book is "Do Right, and God Will Help You" (p. 201). Writing in the first person, Kingsley injected a heavy dose of his religious beliefs into his retellings. He embellished the material found in the ancient sources but did not drastically alter plot lines or tone as Hawthorne did.

Like Hawthorne and Kingsley, Thomas Bulfinch believed that myths should provide pleasure, but he also held that the study of the classical myths was essential to the understanding of English and American literature. In his *The Age of Fable* (1855), written for adults as well as children, Bulfinch strove to retell the myths "correctly, according to the ancient authorities, so that when a reader finds them referred to he may not be at a loss to recognize the reference" (p. vi). Bulfinch added that "such stories and parts of stories as are offensive to pure taste and good morals are not given" (p. vii). Since his main sources were Ovid and Vergil, Bulfinch used the Roman names of characters; and his retellings have the light, graceful tone of the Roman writings rather than the somber religious intensity found in many ancient Greek works.

While Bulfinch stressed the relationship between classical literature and modern literature, other nineteenth century authors linked mythology and other disciplines. The influence of the comparative mythology scholar, Friedrich Max Müller, who concluded in *Comparative Mythology* (1856) that the classical myths are merely metaphoric expressions of solar phenomena, is apparent in George W. Cox's *A Manual of Mythology in the Form of Question and Answer* (1868). In *Classic Myths* (1896), Mary Catherine Judd gave teachers suggestions for combining nature study (the introduction of which into the curriculum had been advocated by Horace Mann) and mythology. Her prefatory comments reveal that Judd, like many of her contemporaries, was a romantic at heart:

> If these stories help to attract children to the beautiful in Nature, or lead them to listen more often to the voices whispering from leaf, wave, or star; or cause them to lose some of their dread of Nature's sterner tones and coarse-forms; then the mission of this book will be fulfilled (preface, n.p.).

Flora Cooke produced *Nature Myths and Stories for Little Children* (1895), a book intended for use in grades 1-3. In choosing myths to include in her elementary reader, *Stories from Plato and Other Classical Writers* (1895), Mary E. Burt selected those which either taught fine moral points or were metaphysical expressions of natural phenomena. Mythological accounts formed a substantial part of the following elementary history texts: *Young Folks' History of Greece* by Charlotte M. Yonge (1878), *The Story of the Greeks* by H. A. Guerber (1896), and *Stories of Greek Gods, Heroes, and Men: A Primer of the Mythology and History of the Greeks* by Caroline H. and Samuel B. Harding (1897). In their preface, the Hardings stress the value of the Greek myths in developing both the child's imagination and his/her sense of ethics.

With the advent of compulsory education laws during the last quarter of the nineteenth century, more children, girls as well as boys, attended school; and the main system of education shifted from private to public. At the turn of the century, the study of mythology was still being combined with the study of history but with a new emphasis--on heroes. In the preface to their *Famous Men of Greece* (1904), John H. Haaren and A. B. Poland, both superintendents of public schools in New York, pointed out that good pedagogy dictated that the study of history begin with biography because history only holds the child's attention when it presents personages with whom the child may identify (n.p.). Mary E. Burt believed that the study of heroes provided role models. In the preface of *Herakles, the Hero of Thebes and Other Heroes of the Myth* (1900), she wrote,

> The rapidity of action in the stories of Herakles, Jason, and other Heroes of the Myth, the prowess and courage and untiring endurance of the men, render the characters worthy subjects of thought to young minds, and have secured the stories a permanent place in educational literature. It is not elegant literature alone that boys need, but inspiring ideals which will impel them to stand fearlessly to their guns, to do the hard thing with untiring perseverance, to reach the result with unerring insight (p. v).

Between 1900 and 1910, many books on ancient heroes appeared. These included *Heroes of Myth and Legend* by Benjamin Ide Wheeler (1903), *Heroes of the Olden Time* by Pamela McArthur Cole (1904), *Hero Tales Told in School* (a reader) by James Baldwin (1907), and *Heroes Every Child Should Know* by Hamilton Wright Mabie (1907). The fact that Mabie's book included both Perseus and Robert E. Lee suggests that the interest in heroes was partly generated by Civil War stories such as Stephen Crane's *The Red Badge of Courage*, which had been published in 1895. Tales of the Civil War and reports of Heinrich Schliemann's excavations of the ruins at Troy during the 1890s probably helped create an interest in Trojan War myths. In 1900, W. P. Trent produced an edition of Charles Lamb's *The Adventures of Ulysses*, which itself was a paraphrased and abridged children's version of Chapman's famous translation of the *Odyssey*. In 1907, Andrew Lang published *Tales of Troy and Greece*. Between 1900 and 1925, the World War I era, Walter Copland Perry produced *The Boy's Iliad* (1902) and *The Boy's Odyssey* (1901), while Alfred A. Church wrote both adult and children's versions of the *Iliad* (1907), the *Odyssey* (1906), and the *Aeneid* (1908). Agnes Cook Gale wrote *The Children's Odyssey* (1912); Padraic Colum, *The Adventures of Odysseus and the Tale of Troy* (1918).

Elementary school readers, such as *Myths of Old Greece in Story and Song* by William Adams (1900) and *Stories of Long Ago in a New Dress* by Grace H. Kupfer (1908) showed the influence of Bulfinch, for they combined the retelling of ancient myths with thematically related selections from modern literature. In *The Great Stories of the Greeks* (1904), Lilian Stoughton Hyde presented Greek myths "that have been world favorites through the centuries and that in some measure exercised a formative influence in the literature and fine arts in many communities" (p. iii).

Between 1910 and 1920, the trends of the first decade of the twentieth century continued and new trends appeared. Corinne Spickelmire's comments on bards and the Homeric Question in *Stories of Hellas* (1911) correspond to the research topics of the classical scholars of the time. Suggesting a new interest in the education of women and the movement for the suffrage of women, which was flourishing then, is a book entitled *Heroines That Every Child Should Know* by Hamilton Wright Mabie and Kate Stephens (1911). Indicative of the fact that nature study was still considered important are two textbooks: *Nature Myths of Many Lands* by Florence Virginia Farmer (1910) and *The Wonder Garden* by Frances Jenkins Olcott (1919). Olcott's book contains suggestions for teachers, including a model program for teaching nature myths. Farmer's book is a reader.

The widening of the elementary school curriculum by the addition of such subjects as drawing, music, and manual arts resulted from a change in educational philosophy. One of the main advocates of the new progressive education was John Dewey, who in *The School and Society* (1899) and *The*

Child and the Curriculum (1902) had called for an end to authoritarian teaching methods and to extensive memorization. Influenced by both the fledgling science of psychology, especially the Freudian School, and the pragmatism of William James, Dewey emphasized "learning by doing," which makes the subject matter personally meaningful to the student. He called for the integration of in-school and out-of-school activities, which requires the involvement of both parents and teachers in the educational process. A few progressive educators, though not Dewey, believed that education should be entertaining and not overly intellectually taxing. Some of the aforementioned tendencies can be seen in mythology books produced in the 1920s. At the end of *Four Old Greeks* (1926), Jennie Hall provided teaching suggestions, one of which was that students dramatize the stories. Muriel Kinney, in *Stars and Their Stories* (1926), began with a note to children, urging them to begin with the current month and to study the star groups one at a time. She followed this with a note to parents, suggesting that they point out constellations to their children and then read the appropriate selection with them. Two prefaces, one addressed to the child and the other to the teacher (or parent), are also found in Jane Black's *Mythology for Young People* (1925) and William Byron Forbush's *Myths and Legends of Greece and Rome* (1928). In *Greek Tales for Tiny Tots* (1929), a book to be read to rather than by small children, John Raymond Crawford wrote in a witty, colloquial manner, often adding superfluous and anachronistic details.   According to Crawford, after Perseus married Andromeda, he gave her "a five pound box of chocolates every morning for breakfast" (p. 46). The tone of this book fits the stereotypical image of the "roaring twenties" as a prosperous, carefree, slightly wacky era of Fords and flappers, not to mention the Charleston. Music was an important part of the '20s. At the end of *Orpheus With His Lute* (a new edition of which appeared in 1926), Winifred Margaret Lambart Hutchinson commented on the immortality of music, then quoted lines 105-108 of Milton's *Il Penseroso*. Hutchinson presented a biography of an Orpheus driven by the desire, even as a child, to move people through the power of music. (Note the psychological overtones.)

Experiments in progressive education continued into the 1930s. In her preface to *Council of the Gods* (1981), a novelette into which were woven descriptions of the twelve Olympians and quotations from literature, Ruth Harshaw stated that her book had been tested in the fifth grade of the schools in Winnetka, Illinois (a suburb of Chicago). She related that her aims were first, "to hold the child's interest"; second, "to give a unified picture of Greek mythology"; and third, "to introduce children to poetry with classical themes" (p. vii). In the preface to *Gods, Heroes, and Men of Ancient Greece* (1934), William Henry Denham Rouse noted, "These stories were told to boys ten to eleven years old, and they have gained by the boys' criticism, conscious and unconscious" (p. vii). Using first-person narrative for comments and explanations, Rouse wrote as a storyteller addressing a young audience. His reference to evolution from monkeys (p. 13) brings to mind the Scopes trial of

1925 and its effect on education. The era's fascination with flying, possibly inspired by Charles A. Lindbergh's solo flight across the Atlantic in 1927, was appealed to in *Wonder Flights of Long Ago* by Mary Elizabeth Barry and Paul R. Hanna (1930). Intended as a reader for the intermediate grades, the book provided teachers with suggested activities and included a sample dramatization of the story of Daedalus. Eleanor Farjeon's *Mighty Men from Achilles to Julius Caesar* (1930) combined history, myth, and modern poetry.

During the 1930s children's literature gradually shifted away from classics, primarily to things American. Several factors contributed to the change in focus. The Great Depression that followed the Stock Market Crash of 1929 caused Americans to turn their attention to domestic matters. The widening of the elementary school curriculum left less time for Classical Studies. After the turn of the century, realism, with an American focus, became a characteristic of adult art and literature. In 1930, Sinclair Lewis, famous for his muckraking novels about urban life in the United States, won the Nobel Prize for Literature and Grant Wood exhibited *American Gothic*. There was one notable exception: in 1934 Paul Manship completed the bronze Prometheus Fountain in Rockefeller Center in New York.

The movement away from classical literature continued into the 1940s. During the '40s very few children's books on classical mythology were published. Of these, two were simplifications of Bulfinch's work. Prometheus, a symbol of revolt against tyranny, figured prominently in another three: Janette Sebring Lowrey's *In the Morning of the World* (1944), Catharine F. Sellew's *Adventures with the Gods* (1946), and Beatrice Alexander's *Famous Myths of the Golden Age* (1947). Reflecting the hardships created by World War II, Lowrey centered her book around the idea (not found in ancient sources) that Zeus ordered Prometheus to create men suited to live during a Golden Age but that Prometheus dreamed of and then created men who by their "capacity for enduring toil and pain and sorrow would be able to substitute for the ease and pleasure of a vanished age, intelligence, courage, and nobility" (p. 25). In the *Stars in Our Heaven: Myths and Fables* (1948), Peter Lum combined astronomical and mythological materials.

In the 1950s interest in classical mythology revived. As the title of *Greek Stories for Pleasure Reading* by Edward W. Dolch et al. (1955) suggests, in the '50s emphasis was often placed on the entertainment value of the Greek myths. Many authors strove to present traditional stories in new ways. Inspired by Andrew Lang's retelling of the myth of Perseus as a fairy tale in *The Blue Fairy Book* (1889), Roger Lancelyn Green, having searched out Greek myths with fairy tale motifs, wrote *Old Greek Fairy Tales* (1958). Green eliminated as many character names as possible and reproduced the style in which fairy tales were written. In *Mystery at Mycenae* (1959), Green presented a who-done-it for pre-teens. The mystery had a twentieth century tone though the subject was ancient--the abduction of Helen by Theseus. Tom Galt's *Rise of the Thunderer*

(1954) was similar in tone to a modern paperback romance. The following passage describes the first meeting of Uranus and Gaia:

> Uranus's face was calm. His midnight hair drifted about his regal head casually, disdainfully, lifted by a gentle breeze. Wearing a belt of stars, he rode the sky in king-like majesty.
>
> Eagerly she watched him. Slowly his eyelids opened, and his eyes glanced out mysteriously, darkly.
>
> Great Uranus gazed, she thought, at her. And then he sighed, with such a happy sigh as evening shadows sometimes, lisp, welcoming the delights of sleep (p. 3).

In *The Adventures of Ulysses* (1959), Gerald Gottlieb made Elpenor a character of greater significance than he is in the *Odyssey*. Though she never mentioned her source, Shirley Barker, in *The Trojan Horse* (1959), followed Vergil's account but took the side of the Greeks, making Sinon the hero of her story. Frederick J. Moffitt had Odysseus keep a diary on his way home from Troy. The adaptation of ancient Greek and Roman myths into pre-teen novelettes mirrored what was occurring in the adult entertainment world. In 1950, Jacques Cocteau directed his film *Orphei*; in 1951, Howard Fast published *Spartacus* (a mythologized account of an historical character), which was made into both a movie and ballet. Romantic love was as prominent a theme in these adult works as it was in children's literature of the period. Olivia Coolidge, in *The Trojan War* (1952), highlighted the marriage of Peleus and Thetis, the love of Oenone for Paris, and the reunion of Odysseus and Penelope. Entertaining literature provided escape from the realities of the Korean War and the tension of the cold war. When the USSR launched Sputnik in 1959, the race to the moon, which dominated the next decade, began.

The 1960s was an age of heroes: the astronauts, Martin Luther King, and John Kennedy were idolized. As might be expected, there appeared a good number of children's books on ancient heroes, including *Greek Gods and Heroes* by Robert Graves (1960), *Adventures of the Greek Heroes* by Mollie McLean and Anne Wiseman (1961), and a new edition of Kingsley's *The Heroes* (1968). Two books--*Giants, Dragons and Gods: Constellations and Their Folklore* (1968) by Dirk Gringhuis and *Heavenly Zoo* (1963) by Howard Stanley Aronson--combined astronomical and mythological information. The pre-teen novelette remained popular. Flying was involved in four: *A White Horse With Wings* (1968) by Anthea Davies, *Phaëthon* (1966) by Merrill Pollack, *A Fall From the Sky: The Story of Daedalus* (1966) and *The Gorgon's Head: The Story of Perseus* (1962) by Ian Serraillier. The popularity of the movie *Bell, Book, and Candle* (1958) and of Arthur Miller's drama *The Crucible* (1959) produced a fascination with witchcraft that endured throughout much of the next decade. The theme occurs in several children's books of the period. One such work was Jacynth Hope-Simpson's *A Cavalcade of Witches* (1967), which included Medea.

As evidenced by Florence Marie Gerdes' *The Aeneid: A Retelling for Young People* (1969), the Trojan War continued to be a favorite theme in the '60s--even throughout the Vietnam War years.

Several '60s authors wove a substantial amount of archaeological information into their stories. For example, Serraillier wove descriptions of Cretan sites into his novelette about Daedalus. In the epilogue of *Farewell to Troy* (1964), Dorothy M. Johnson told her young readers about the ruins of Troy and about ancient literature on the Trojan War. Since the significance of the art of writing is an important theme in her story, she also gave the history of the alphabet. One wonders if the excitement caused by Michael Ventris' decipherment of Linear B, a Minoan syllabary, in 1952 played a part in inspiring the book. During the decade of the 1960s, collections of stories were more popular than books on individual myths.

While the university riots of the late '60s and early '70s resulted in a movement away from traditional courses of study, children's books on mythology became more scholarly. Writers tended to follow their ancient sources conscientiously, adding only bits of descriptive detail. Penelope Proddow produced translations of several *Homeric Hymns*. Marilynne K. Roach's *Two Roman Mice* (1975) is a translation of Horace, *Satires II, 6*. Lanzo Anderson, in *Arion and the Dolphins* (1978), retold, in simple language, the Herodotean account. Despite some bowdlerization, Edna Barth remained faithful to Apuleius' tale of Cupid and Psyche in her *Cupid and Psyche: A Love Story* (1976). The description of the Gorgons in Margaret Hodges' *The Gorgon's Head: A Myth from the Isles of Greece* (1972) is taken directly from Apollodorus, *Library* 2.4.2. Carefully weaving together material from various ancient sources, Doris Gates produced a series of biographies of Olympian deities. Perhaps inspired by the title of Robert Graves' adult novel *I Claudius*, which was made into a television series in 1976, Elizabeth Silverthorne offered *I Heracles* (1978), an autobiography of the hero. Two books, Gabriel Deblander's *The Fall of Icarus* (1978), which was based on Pieter Brueghel's painting of the same name, and Penelope Proddow's *Art Tells a Story: Greek and Roman Myths* (1977), focused on the relationship between mythology and art as did Edna Barth's *Hearts, Cupids, and Red Roses: The Story of the Valentine Symbols* (1976).

The nudity craze, exemplified by the appearance of the drama *Oh! Calcutta* in 1969 and the unexpected appearance of streakers at various events in 1974, was, strangely enough, reflected in children's literature. The first edition of Doris Gates' *Two Queens of Heaven* (1974) had eye-catching illustrations that featured topless goddesses, illustrations which were somehow more disquieting than the traditional classic nude figures. The same tendency may be seen in some of the illustrations in *The God Beneath the Sea: A Recreation of the Greek Legends* (1971) by Leon Garfield and Edward Blishen. Reflecting the free-love movement of the late '60s and early '70s, this book contains several somewhat explicit love-making scenes.

Gates' books on female goddesses, the first of a kind, reveal another phenomenon of the 1970s--the growth of the women's movement. Demeter, the Olympian deity who best typifies the earth-mother goddess stereotype, became especially popular. Between 1971 and 1974, five female writers--Sarah F. Tomaino, Penelope Proddow, Penelope Farmer, Margaret Hodges, and Doris Gates--retold her story.

In the 1970s interest turned from science to science fiction. In 1977, the year in which George Lucas directed *Star Wars*, Lawrence and Irene Swinburne published *Ancient Myths: The First Science Fiction*, in which they compared ancient heroes to bionic heroes. *Mythical Monsters* by James Cornell (1973) and *Mythological Creatures: A Pictorial Dictionary* by Paulita Sedgwick (1974) were precursors of the monster mania spawned by the popularity of the game Dungeons and Dragons.

While enrollments in Greek and Latin at the higher levels of education plummeted in the late '70s and '80s, experimental courses at the elementary-school level became more widespread. In the '80s the number of children's books on classical mythology was more than double that of the previous decade. As a rule, however, the books were smaller in size and more limited in focus. Series of books, such as the thirteen volume survey entitled *Greek Mythology* by Menelaos Stephanides (actually begun in the '70s), appeared in lieu of collections. These tendencies befitted the age of *Sesame Street*, quality time, half-hour sitcoms, and microwave ovens. Indicative of the love of brevity was *One-Minute Greek Myths* (1987) by the puppeteer Shari Lewis, a book which provided busy parents with stories to read to their children. In the hope of fostering cultural literacy, William F. Russell wrote *Classic Myths to Read Aloud* (1989). He indicated the estimated reading time of each story and included etymological commentary.

In the 1980s the most popular mythological subject was the Trojan War, with an emphasis on Odysseus. I. M. Richardson in *The Wooden Horse: The Fall of Troy* (1984), Catherine Storr in *The Trojan Horse* (1985), and Peter Connolly in *The Legend of Odysseus* (1986) briefly retold the story of the Trojan War. In his book, Connolly analyzed the myth of Odysseus from an archaeological point of view. He discussed archaeological finds at the end of each section of his narrative. Like Connolly's book, Emily Little's *The Trojan Horse: How the Greeks Won the War* (1988)--designed for use in grades 2-4--combined both mythological and archaeological information. Richardson's book was part of a series of six books, each of which focused on a part of Homer's *Odyssey*. John Norwood Fazo produced textbooks of the *Iliad* and the *Odyssey* in comic book format. A "Words to Know" list and study questions were placed at the end of each text, and there were footnotes throughout. In 1981, Diana Stewart presented condensed versions of the *Iliad* and the *Odyssey*. In the same year, Vivian Webb and Heather Amery wrote *The Amazing*

Adventures of Ulysses. Emily Frenkel's retelling of the *Aeneid* appeared in 1986.

Perhaps influenced by the structuralism of Claude Lévi-Strauss, who in his search for oppositions in myth considered all versions of myths equally valid, and by the deconstructionism of Jacques Derrida, who held that texts have no definitely identifiable meaning or value--or in some cases perhaps because authors lacked the thorough knowledge of literary works gained through reading them in their original language, several writers of children's mythology books in the 1980s altered essential details of the myths. The '80s movie, *Clash of the Titans*, did the same thing; for in that film Perseus, not Bellerophontes, rode Pegasus. Making radical changes in story lines and adding a host of new characters and plots, Bernard Evslin, in a plethora of books, rewrote classical mythology to his own liking. For example, in Evslin's *Cyclopes*, Ulysses tries to stop his men from entering the cave of the Cyclops Polyphemus. Confronted by Polyphemus, who is at home, Odysseus volunteers to do corrective surgery to provide the Cyclops with an additional eye and attractive facial features. When Polyphemus agrees to the surgery, Ulysses gives him wine as an anesthetic, then clunks him over the head with a mallet to render him unconscious. In Homer's *Odyssey*, it is Odysseus who wishes to wait for the absent owner of the cave and to receive gifts from him. After getting Polyphemus drunk with wine, Odysseus, aided by his men, gouges out the Cyclops' eye with a hot stake.

While Evslin's books are offensive to the classicist because they give children reading the myths for the first time a false picture, Peggy Thompson's parody, *The King Has Horse's Ears* (1988) is not because all of the names as well as the historic setting are changed. It is interesting to note that in the decade of clever, self-aggrandizing men with a passion for possessions, notably Donald Trump, Jim Bakker, Michael Milken, and Ivan Boesky, several children's books on Midas and the golden touch appeared, for example, *The Story of King Midas* by Pamela Espeland (1980) and *King Midas and the Golden Touch* by Katherine Hewitt (1987). One will also remember that cleverness and a desire for possessions play a prominent part in the story of Odysseus, the decade's favorite mythological character.

The '80s fascination with men confronting monsters--from the lovable E.T. to the monsters in Dungeons and Dragons and video games to the nasty Gremlins--was reflected in the great number of children's books on ancient heroes, many of which mention monsters in their titles. C. J. Naden, Catherine Storr, and Leonard Everett Fisher all composed books entitled *Theseus and the Minotaur*. Naden also produced *Perseus and Medusa* (1981), while Will and Mary Pope Osborne offered *The Deadly Power of Medusa* (1988). Some of the above are actually biographies of heroes. William Wise called his collection of hero myths *Monster Myths of Ancient Greece* (1981). Evslin turned out a series of twenty-one books on the monsters of classical mythology. In the '80s, adventure films, including *Raiders of the Lost Ark*, which involved archaeology achieved great popularity. In the area of children's books, Heracles, Jason, Bellerophontes, and Cadmus each had at least one book written about his adventures.

Possibly because of the suggestion of an unseen monster in the myth, not only did two individual books on the love story of Eros and Psyche--*The Adventures of Eros and Psyche* (1983) and *The Arrow and the Lamp* (1989)--appear; but Mary Pope Osborne added the story to the tales from Ovid she retold in *Favorite Greek Myths* (1989). Another love story, that of Pygmalion, provided both the subject of a children's book, *The Story of Pygmalion* by Pamela Espeland (1981) and the theme for a film, *Pretty Woman*, which was made in the late 1980s and appeared in 1990.

In the '90s, interest in classical mythology is still flourishing. Apropos of this age of audio and video cassettes, some books come with audio-visual materials. One example is Robert Newby's *King Midas: With Select Sentences in American Sign Language* (1990), a retelling of Hawthorne's version of the myth in word and in sign language, in print and on videotape. Another is *King Midas and the Golden Touch* by Eric Metaxas (1992), which includes an audio cassette with narration and music. Perhaps the '90s nostalgic interest in deceased musicians, as evidenced by the appearance of a play about Buddy Holly and a movie about Jim Morrison as well as by the commemoration of Elvis Presley with a postage stamp, at least in part provided the inspiration for *Orpheus* by Charles Mikolaycak (1992).

The effect of cleverness untempered with kindness (cf. George Bush's political objective of a "kinder, gentler nation") is explored in Jane Yolen's *Wings*, which focuses on the reactions of the deities to Daedalus' hubristic actions. That the Trojan War has retained its popularity as a subject for children's books is suggested by Elizabeth Edmondson's *The Trojan War* (1992) and Leonard Everett Fisher's *Cyclops* (1991). Books for younger children have appeared in greater numbers recently, for example, *Greek and Roman Mythology A to Z: A Young Reader's Companion* by Kathleen N. Daly (1992). Jamie and Scott Simons have authored a series of picture books of etiological myths, including *Why Spiders Spin: A Story of Arachne* (1991) and *Why Winter Comes: A Story of Persephone* (1991). New books appear regularly--each affected in some way by the changing times.

In summary, myths, though timeless, reflect the historical and social context in which they are told. Though knowledge of the context is not essential to the understanding of the myth proper, it greatly enhances both the understanding and appreciation of each particular retelling.

References and Uncited Sources

Note: For bibliographic information on children's books mentioned in this chapter, see the Annotated Bibliography.

Anthon, Charles. *A Classical Dictionary, Containing an Account of the Principal Proper Names Mentioned in Ancient Authors, and Intended to Elucidate All the Important Points Connected With the Geography, History, Mythology, and Fine Arts of the Greeks and Romans.* 4th ed. New York: Harper and Brothers, 1845.

Arbuthnot, May Hill and Sutherland, Zena. *Children and Books.* Glenview, Ill.: Scott, Foresman and Company, 1972.

Bingham, Jan and Scholt, Grayce. *Fifteen Centuries of Children's Literature: An Annotated Chronology of British and American Works in Historical Context.* Westport, Conn.: Greenwood Press, 1980.

Crane, Stephen. *The Red Badge of Courage.* New York: The Modern Library, 1894.

Dewey, John. *The Child and the Curriculum.* Chicago, Ill.: University of Chicago Press, 1906.

Dewey, John. *The School and Society.* Chicago, Ill.: University of Chicago Press, 1900.

Fast, Howard. *Spartacus.* New York: Crown Publishers, 1951.

Feldman, Burton and Richardson, Robert D. *The Rise of Modern Mythology 1680-1860.* Bloomington: Indiana University Press, 1972.

Fogle, Richard Harter. *Hawthorne's Fiction: The Light and the Dark Period.* Norman: University of Oklahoma Press, 1964.

Georgiou, Constantine. *Children and Their Literature.* Englewood Cliffs, New Jersey: Prentice-Hall, 1969.

Graves, Robert. *I Claudius.* New York: Avon Publishers, 1934.

Hathaway, Richard D. "Hawthorne and the Paradise of Children." *Western Humanities* 15 (1961): 161-172.

Homer. *The Odyssey.* 2 vols. Translated by George Chapman. With introduction and notes by Richard Hooper. London: R. J. Smith, 1857.

Lathrop, Rose Hawthorne. *Memories of Hawthorne.* Boston: Houghton, Mifflin and Company, 1897.

McPherson, Hugo. *Hawthorne as Myth-Maker: A Study in Imagination.* Toronto: University of Toronto Press, 1969.

McPherson, Hugo. "Hawthorne Major Sources for his Mythological Tales." *American Literature* 30: 364-365.

Meigs, Cornelia Lynde, ed. *A Critical History of Children's Literature.* New York: Macmillan, 1969.

Müller, Friedrich Max. *Comparative Mythology*. London: G. Routledge and
Sons, 1909.
Times in Review: 1960-1969. New York: Times, 1970.
Urdang, Laurence, ed. *Tables of American History*. New York: Simon and
Schuster, 1981.

The Retelling of
Myths to Children:
Methodologies

In the process of reviewing children's books on ancient Greek and Roman mythology, one finds several methods of composition employed, each dependent on the author's attitude toward the mythic tradition. The most direct method and the one which best preserves the integrity of an ancient source, is to present a simplified and abridged but close translation of a particular work of literature. Many books based on classical epics employ this method. Penelope Proddow has produced translations of several *Homeric Hymns* (see Annotated Bibliography). A second method of preserving traditional accounts is that of offering a paraphrase or summary of a myth as it is told in ancient sources. Most dictionaries and encyclopedias of mythology for children do this.

Another method of composition is to simulate a historical romance which reflects the attitudes, values, and manners of a particular non-classical age--often the age in which the author is living. The author changes the tone of the original work by creating new conversations, incidents, and even new characters (usually minor ones). Descriptive passages abound, and anachronisms are common. Nathaniel Hawthorne popularized this method. Having found the tone of the classical myths too cold for his taste, he gave the myths a warmer, more romantic quality. In his retellings, characters express their emotions freely. Events are described in minute detail. The hero's faults are minimized while his virtues are extolled. The Anglican cleric Charles Kingsley, retelling the classic myths for his children, injected his personal religious sentiments into his famous work on the Greek heroes. Tom Galt's *The Rise of the Thunderer* has a tone similar to that of a Barbara Cartland novel. In *The Gods in Winter*, Patricia Miles sets the story of Demeter (alias Mrs. Korngold) in the 1970s.

A third method is to build on the basic framework of a myth, especially one sketchily told in ancient accounts. This method is frequently employed in creating a biography of a hero. Information from several sources is blended into one coherent story. Descriptive details, particularly in confrontation and escape scenes, are invented. Psychological insights are provided. At its best, this method results in a complete picture not found in any one source. Doris Gates presents a comprehensive portrait of a deity in *The Golden God: Apollo*. At its worst, the method creates a hybrid not essentially true to any of its sources. Retellings of creation myths are prone to this problem. When two famous versions of a myth are blended, a person well-grounded in the classics immediately intuits what the ancients meant when they spoke of the *contaminatio* effected by Roman playwrights who combined several Greek dramas into one new work.

The final method used in writing books on classical mythology for children is to use mythological characters and situations to create entirely new myths or to add to an existing saga. In Dorothy M. Johnson's *Farewell to Troy*, a fictitious grandson of Priam relates his adventures during and after the fall of Troy. Some authors who use this method are more interested in mythopoesis than in the preservation of the classical tradition. From the classicist's viewpoint, abuse of this method occurs when an author arbitrarily changes incidents and even traits of characters to make them fit into the story he or she has created.

The composition methods just described are employed both in monographs and in collections of myths, where another factor plays an important part--the arrangement of the myths. Many collections are divided into sections devoted to various topics: deities, monsters, influence of classical mythology on some aspect of modern life or literature, etc. Sometimes authors imitate the Ovidian technique of weaving one myth into another. Sometimes they work classical myths into a fictional contemporary setting.

The formats of children's books on ancient Greek and Roman mythology vary as much as the methods of composition. They include autobiographies, biographies, comic books, coffee-table books (picture books), coloring books, dictionaries (encyclopedias) of mythology, dramas, novelettes, and elementary-school readers.

Whatever the method of composition or format, the classicist takes delight in those books which excite interest in the ancient Greek and Roman myths without seriously disfiguring their storyline and tone.

Annotated Bibliography

Please note: Grade level is indicated at the end of each annotation. Unless indicated otherwise, references to Ovid are to his *Metamorphoses*. For a discussion of ancient sources of myth, see Preface.

1. Adams, William. *Myths of Old Greece in Story and Song*. Book III of the Lakeside Literature Series. New York: American Book Company, 1900.

    In the preface to this reader which is intended to serve as an introduction to classical mythology, Adams states that he strove "to present the stories essentially according to the traditions" (p. 3) while preserving the spirit of the myths. Adams omits unessential names and incidents but adds narrative details if the original account is sparse. He treats of the major gods and heroes and includes simplified versions of the *Iliad* and the *Odyssey*. At the end of each chapter in the book, there is a poem on a classical theme, for example, Longfellow's "Pegasus in Pound." The book's thorough index has annotations and a pronunciation guide. Captioned line drawings show critical scenes. 6+

2. Alexander, Beatrice (pseudonym of Louise Raymond). *Famous Myths of the Golden Age*. Illustrated by Florian. New York: Random House, 1947.

    This introduction to classical mythology begins with comments on the ancient Greek view of the universe. Each chapter presents a well-known story, retold with some modifications; for example,

Ulysses has his ears filled with wax so that he will *not* hear the song of the Sirens. Large, lively illustrations, many in color, and large print make the book especially attractive.   4+

3.   Anderson, Lonzo. *Arion and the Dolphins.* Illustrated by Adrienne Adams. New York: Charles Scribner's Sons, 1978.

Anderson retells, in simple language, the Herodotean account of Arion. He adds to the end of the legend, giving it a more definite conclusion. Small amounts of text are superimposed over double-page illustrations in watercolor tones.   4+

4.   Aronson, Howard Stanley. *Heavenly Zoo.* San Antonio: The Naylor Company, 1963.

This slim volume contains much mythological and scientific information about the signs of the zodiac and other constellations.   Star maps indicate the positions of the astral configurations during the various seasons. Aronson gives concise versions of the myths but includes all the essential details found in ancient sources.   Mythological explanations of Capricorn, Aquarius, and Pisces are not presented although the physical appearance of each of those constellations is described.   6+

5.   Baker, Emilie Kip. *Stories of Old Greece and Rome.* New York: The Macmillan Company, 1913.

Baker's book contains all of the major classical myths and hero stories except those concerning the Trojan War; the story of the apple of discord is included, however. In telling the story of Pandora, Baker relies heavily on Hawthorne's account (see Hawthorne, *A Wonder Book*), but in the rest of the book she remains true to the ancient sources. The impressive appendices provide explanatory material, both literary and cultural; give modern and ancient sources of myths; and discuss relevant ancient works of art, some of which are subjects of the book's black and white illustrations. The index is very thorough, and there is a list of Roman deities (Baker used the Roman names) with their Greek counterparts. The better the student, the more he or she will be able to derive from this book.   6+

6.   Baldwin, James. *The Golden Fleece: More Old Greek Stories*. New
        York: American Book Company, 1905.

        This book differs from other books on the Argonautic expedition in that
        it provides a great deal of background information, which is woven into
        the story of Cretheus, Jason's grandfather. In his epilogue, Baldwin
        reveals that he borrowed from many sources but also employed his own
        fancy, adding and omitting as he saw fit (pp. 285-286). This practice,
        which results in some seeming inaccuracies will send the experienced
        classicist to check the ancient sources (nowhere indicated by the author)
        but will not disturb the neophyte. Baldwin's narrative flows very
        smoothly, and the black and white illustrations are closely connected
        with the text. A pronunciation guide is included.   4+

7.   Baldwin, James. *Hero Tales Told in School*. New York: Charles
        Scribner's Sons, 1907.

        Originally intended for use in reading classes, this book contains
        selections from several of Baldwin's works on epic heroes.
        Representing classical mythology are nine stories from the author's *A
        Story of the Golden Age* (see below). These include "The Hunt in the
        Wood of Calydon," "The Choice of Heracles," and "Paris and
        Helen."   6+

8.   Baldwin, James. *Old Greek Stories*. New York: American Book
        Company, 1895.

        In his preface, Baldwin states that his intention is to retell the classical
        myths "simply as stories" (p. 3) with no interpretation and no
        references to the supernatural (the gods are referred to as Mighty
        Beings or kings). Baldwin generally follows the ancient accounts. He
        often chooses a lesser known version of a myth; for example, following
        Apollodorus' account, he has Persephone order Shadow Leader to bring
        Alcestis back to the upper world. The tales are presented in such a
        way that they may be read either as a continuing narrative or
        independently. Subjects include Prometheus, Io, Cadmus, Perseus, and
        Theseus. Quotations from the text appear under the major illustrations
        (fine line drawings). The book is bound in blue cloth, stamped in black
        and yellow. Language is kept simple, and there is a pronunciation
        guide.   4+

9.   Baldwin, James. *A Story of the Golden Age.* Illustrated by Howard
        Pyle. New York: Charles Scribner's Sons, 1924 (originally published
        in 1887).

        In his foreword, Baldwin states, "My object in writing . . . has been
        to pave the way to an enjoyable reading of Homer" (p. viii). He
        presents a partial biography of Odysseus, which extends from the
        hero's birth to the stealing of the Palladion. Several chapters are
        devoted to Odysseus' visit with his grandfather Autolycus. Into his
        smooth-flowing continuous narrative, Baldwin weaves many myths
        about characters important in the Trojan War saga, including Achilles,
        Paris, Iphigenia, and Apollo. Though, because of the format which he
        has chosen, Baldwin cannot name his sources, he is conscientious in
        following rather closely the accounts given in primary sources. In the
        explanatory notes at the end of the book, he does give a few quotations
        from and references to Homer's epics. Captioned full-page black and
        white illustrations aid understanding as do the detailed map of Hellas,
        the notes, and the annotated index of proper names.   6+

10.   Baldwin, James. *The Wonder Book of Horses.* New York: The
        Century Company, 1903.

        The majority of stories in this book concern horses familiar to the
        classicist. There are chapters on Helios' horses, Aidoneus' horses,
        Pegasus, Bucephalus, Cyllarus, Harpagus, Balios and Xanthos, and the
        Wooden Horse. The myth of Poseidon's creation of the horse and that
        of the dancing horses of Sybaris are also included. The book features
        an explanatory index and black and white illustrations of horses in
        action. In a note (p. ix), Baldwin states that he selected stories with
        both educative value and intrinsic charm. Through simplified and
        embellished, his retellings do not stray too far from the originals.   4+

11.   Banks, Lynne Reid (see Reid Banks, Lynne).

12.   Barber, Richard W. *A Companion to World Mythology.* Illustrated by
        Pauline Baynes. New York: Delacorte Press, 1979.

        This short encyclopedia of world mythology includes all of the major
        characters of Greek and Roman mythology and many minor ones as
        well. Illustrations, some colored and many based on works of art, are
        placed next to the relevant entries (Captioned or numbered illustrations

would have been more helpful). To aid the reader, the editor has
included an index of topics (cow, crossroads, fire, etc.); an index of
minor characters; an index of names of real people and places; an index
of places with which characters are associated; and a selected index of
versions of myths. The map of Greece has no cities indicated while
that of Italy shows only Rome though other cities are mentioned in the
text.   6 +

13.   Barker, Shirley. *The Trojan Horse.* Illustrated by Fritz Kredel. New
        York: Random House, 1959.

        Barker bases her mini-novel of the Trojan Horse on the Vergilian
        account but takes the side of the Greeks, making Sinon the hero. Many
        captioned illustrations are interspersed throughout the text.   6 +

14.   Barry, Mary Elizabeth and Hanna, Paul R. Illustrated by Lynd Ward.
        Wonder Flights of Long Ago. New York: D. Appleton and Company,
        1930.

        Included in this collection of stories about flying are the myths of
        Daedalus, Phaëthon, Bellerophon, and Perseus. Much dialogue and
        descriptive detail and even a few extra characters have been added.
        Intended as a reader for the intermediate grades, the book provides
        teachers with suggested activities (including a sample dramatization of
        part of the Daedalus story). The word study section features a
        pronunciation guide and explanations written especially for children.
        Each chapter has several captioned lithographs. The first letter of each
        chapter is decorated to suggest the appearance of an illuminated
        manuscript. Pegasus graces the cover of the tome.   4 +

15.   Barth, Edna. *Cupid and Psyche: A Love Story.* Illustrated by Ati
        Forberg. New York: The Seabury Press, 1976.

        Barth presents a bowdlerized account of Apuleius' tale, which, despite
        its omissions, is faithful to the original story line. Fanciful wash
        drawings that capture the wistfulness of the main characters are
        scattered throughout the text.   5 +

16.   Barth, Edna. *Hearts, Cupids, and Red Roses: The Story of the Valentine Symbols*. Illustrated by Ursula Arndt. New York: The Seabury Press, 1974.

As one would expect, Barth makes many references to Cupid and Venus in this comprehensive yet light treatment of the Valentine symbols. She includes the myth of Cupid and Psyche as well as several flower myths. Her discussion of the Lupercalia is very good. Charming black and red illustrations serve both to decorate and clarify.   4+

17.   Beckwith, Mary Helen. *In Mythland*. Illustrated by Susanne Lathrop. Boston: Educational Publishing Company, 1896.

This book, which features large print, numerous black and white illustrations, and very simple sentences, contains a dozen famous myths. Except for the story of Pandora, where she follows Hawthorne (see Hawthorne, *A Wonder Book*), Beckwith stays fairly close to the ancient sources. She includes an introductory note on the deities and a pronunciation guide.   3+

18.   Benson, Sally. *Stories of the Gods and Heroes*. Illustrated by Steele Savage. New York: The Dial Press, 1940.

In this book, Benson presents in simpler language the major myths contained in Thomas Bulfinch's *The Age of Fable* (See Bulfinch). Occasionally, as in the stories of creation and Pandora, she rewrites freely, adding much detail. The pronunciation appears in parentheses after the first mention of a particular name. Each chapter has a black and white illustration showing an important scene in that chapter.   5+

19.   Billout, Guy. *Thunderbolt & Rainbow: A Look at Greek Mythology*. Illustrated by Guy Billout. Englewood Cliffs: Prentice-Hall, Inc., 1981.

Billout combines richly colored artistic representations of scenes of modern city life with discussions of the mythological figures which the scenes suggest. For example, an illustration of a subway police officer and a guard dog accompanies the discussion of Hades. The descriptive passages, each only one paragraph in length, set forth the major characteristics of the mythological personages and often contain an abridged version of a pertinent myth. This book makes a good conversation piece for adults as well as for children.   4+

20.   Birrer, Cynthia and Birrer, William. *Song to Demeter*. Illustrated by Cynthia and William Birrer. New York: Lothrop, Lee and Shepard Books, 1987.

This unique book features very colorful and emotion-filled illustrations, which are reproductions of machine-stitched appliqué and embroidery on fabric. They visually tell the myth of Demeter and Persephone. The accompanying text, which runs along the bottom of each page, is a greatly simplified version of the *Homeric Hymn to Demeter*.   3+

21.   Black, Jane. *Mythology for Young People*. New York: Charles Scribner's Sons, 1925.

This compact little book is a dictionary of mythology which contains over 300 entries (with pronunciation indicated), ranging from Acetes to Lethe to Zeus. In her preface, Black explains her methodology: "I have put into the simplest form very brief explanations of the characters and just enough about them to make the children acquainted with the most important names" (n.p.). In some entries, she includes a passage from English literature and/or a bit of interpretation; and, at the beginning of the book, has a note to her young readers about the origin of mythology. Though the entries are in alphabetical order, there is an index. There are no illustrations.   6+

22.   Blyton, Enid. *Tales of Ancient Greece*. Illustrated by Anne and Janet Johnstone. London: Latimer House Limited, n.d.

Despite the title of her book, Blyton uses the Latin rather than the Greek names of deities. She retells sixteen famous myths (most from Ovid) in simple language. In relating the story of Pandora, Blyton follows Hawthorne's version (see Hawthorne, *A Wonder Book*); but in recounting the other myths, she never violates the original story lines, even though she invents details and conversations. Her book features captioned black and white illustrations of scenes described in the text.   4+

23.   Boden, G. H. and D'Almeida, W. Barrington. *Wonder Stories From Herodotus*. Illustrated by H. Granville Fell. New York: Harper and Brothers, 1900.

Writing in a smooth flowing style, the authors retell legends from Herodotus, including Arion and the dolphin, Solon's visit with Croesus, and Polycrates and his signet ring. Herodotus' accounts are expanded by the addition of dialogue and descriptive passages. Carefully drawn richly colored illustrations with borders and captions make the book visually attractive.   7+

24.   Brown, Elizabeth Virginia.   *When the World Was Young*. Yonkers-on-Hudson, New York: World Book Company, 1913.

This supplementary reader was designed to stimulate interest in culture-history and "to build up an idea of the meaning of the acts of life" (preface, p. 3). It contains two short selections on Pan: "Pan and His Pipes" adapted from Bulfinch (see below) and "A Musical Instrument" by Elizabeth Barrett Browning. A chapter on telling time describes both the sun dial and the *clepsydra*. Line drawings help the reader visualize items described in the text.   4+

25.   Brown, George Percival. *Poems for Children: Based on the Greek Myths*. Ilfracombe, N. Devon: Arthur H. Stockwell, Ltd., 1955.

Brown's prefatory poem written in rhymed iambic heptameter, addresses the importance of studying mythology. His opening poem, in the same meter, "The Kingdom of the Father Dyaus," introduces the major deities. (Unfortunately Father Dyaus is never identified either in the poems or in the otherwise fairly complete "Pronouncing and Explanatory Index.") Following are poems based on Hesiod and Ovid. Finally, there is a poetic biography of Hercules. The poems are free retellings of the myths--some, for example, the Hercules poems, follow ancient accounts closely; others, for example, the poem on Narcissus, show great poetic license. From time to time, Brown interrupts his third person narrative to address his young readers.   6+

26.   Bryant, Lorinda Munson. *The Children's Book of Celebrated Legends*.
         New York: The Century Company, 1929.

         Bryant presents a collection of famous works of art on literary themes.
         Fourteen are related to classical mythology. These include *Orpheus
         and Eurydice* by Watts, *Apollo and Daphne* by Bernini, *Daedalus and
         Icarus* by Canova, and *Phaëthon and the Chariot of the Sun* by
         Sargent. Each illustration is paired with a page of commentary on the
         work of art, the myth behind it, and the artist. Bryant's brief retellings
         of the myths are accurate, and she includes alternative versions but
         does not mention her sources. In the introduction, which is addressed
         to children, Bryant discusses the origin of myths and legends.

         Other illustrations include *The Triumph of Galatea* by Raphael, *The
         Pleiades* by Vedder, *The Horses of Achilles* by Regnault, *Hercules
         Killing Nessos* by Pollajuolo, *An Amazon* (statue in Vatican), *The
         Horses of Diomedes* by Borglum, *The Forge of Vulcan* by Tintoretto,
         The Birth of Athena (well-head) *Hope* by Watts, and *Ganymede and the
         Eagle* by Correggio.   8 +

27.   Bryant, Sara Cone (Mrs. Theodore F. Borst). *Best Stories to Tell to
         Children*. Illustrated by Patten Wilson. Boston: Houghton Mifflin
         Company, 1912.

         Included in this collection are the legend of Tarpeia and the myth of the
         judgment of Midas. The latter story is adapted from *Old Greek Folk
         Stories* by Josephine Preston Peabody (see below). The stories are
         retold in simple language with only a small amount of embellishment.
         Though the book has full-page, captioned colored illustrations, none
         accompanies either of the stories discussed here. The book has large
         print.   5 +

28.   Buckley, Elsie Finnimore. *Children of the Dawn: Old Tales of Greece*.
         Illustrated by Frank C. Papé. London: Wills, Gardner, Darton, and
         Co., Ltd., 1908.

         Combining material from various ancient pieces of literature, Buckley
         retells eleven myths, including "The Riddle of the Sphinx," "The Curse
         of Echo," and "Paris and Oenone." She makes some changes in the
         original story lines, especially when bowdlerizing. She adds
         descriptive detail and dialogue. Young readers will find Buckley's
         language somewhat antiquated and her vocabulary a bit sophisticated.

In the introduction to the book, Arthur Sidgwick comments on the myths and their sources as well as on Buckley's methodology. The finely detailed line drawings are visual representations of lines from the text, which are reproduced under the respective illustrations.   8 +

29.   Bulfinch, Thomas. *A Book of Myths: Selections from Bulfinch's Age of Fable.* Illustrated by Helen Sewell. New York: The Macmillan Company, 1942.

This simplified version of Bulfinch's *The Age of Fable* (see next entry) omits some passages which contain unessential details and most references to English literature. It contains the original introduction and fifteen Greek and Roman myths. Simple, clear drawings enhance understanding.

30.   Bulfinch, Thomas. *The Age of Fable.* Boston: Charles E. Brown, 1855 (see next entry).

31.   Bulfinch, Thomas. *Bulfinch's Mythology.* New York: Thomas Y. Crowell Company, 1913.

Although this classic work, which includes all of the major myths in western literature, is geared to older readers, it is often included in children's collections. Bulfinch's retellings of the myths should not cause problems for the young reader with a good vocabulary, but his references to English literature might. Striving to educate as well as to entertain, Bulfinch (as he states in his preface) is careful to tell the stories as the ancient sources did, "so that when the reader finds them referred to he may not be at a loss to recognize the reference" (p. vi). Bulfinch includes an annotated index so that his book may serve as a reference book.

This complete edition includes three works originally published separately: *The Age of Fable* (1855) on classical mythology, *The Age of Chivalry* (1858) on northern mythology, and *The Age of Charlemagne or Romance of the Middle Ages* (1863). It features black and white illustrations. For a book of condensed and simplified selections from *The Age of Fable*, see Bulfinch, Thomas, *A Book of Myths: Selections from Bulfinch's Age of Fable* above.   8 +

32.　Burland, Cottie Arthur. *The Gods and Heroes of War*. Illustrated by Honi Werner. New York: G. P. Putnam's Sons, 1974.

Burland's interest in ethnology and archaeology is evident in this study of the chief warrior gods of four ancient cultures--Aztec, Babylonian, Viking, and Greek. Because Burland believes that "the Greeks saw their war god, as a raving madman" (p. 123) unworthy of admiration (an assessment with which most classicists would not totally agree), he focuses on the mortal hero Achilles in his chapter on the Bronze Age culture of Greece. Burland includes a summary of Homer's *Iliad*, written from a more historical than literary perspective. Achilles' grandfather is called Turomedon rather than Automedon. There are three captioned black and white illustrations (Zeus, Trojan Horse, Ares) in the chapter. 8 +

33.　Burt, Mary E. *Stories from Plato and Other Classic Writers*. Boston: Ginn and Company, 1895.

This book is intended as a reader for children from six to twelve years old. Burt employs a huge amount of creative license in retelling myths; for example, she has Coronis become a crow. At the end of each chapter there are spelling words, a note to teachers about the source of the story, and topics for discussion.

Of the value of the myths, Burt says "These stories I found useful in previous schoolwork, because they contained fine moral points, or else they were poetic statements of natural phenomenon which might enhance the study of natural science" (p. viii). 1-7

34.　Burt, Mary E. and Ragozin, Zenaïde. *Herakles, the Hero of Thebes and Other Heroes of the Myth*. New York: Charles Scribner's Sons, 1900.

In the preface, Burt points out that hero myths always remain popular not only because they feature rapidity of action but also because they provide boys with inspiring ideals. Bowdlerizing much, Burt and Ragozin present mini-biographies of all the major Greek heroes. Their treatment of Herakles is the most exhaustive, of Pelops, the least. They add explanatory comments, for example, on the duties of the charioteer and on the importance of hospitality, which provide insights into ancient Greek culture. They also include descriptions of famous places. Most of their material comes from ancient sources, but they invent narrative details. The book in an adaptation of the second book of the primary schools of Athens, Greece, c. 1900. Most of the illustrations (in black and white) show famous works of art. There is a pronunciation guide.   6+

35.   Burt, Mary E. and Ragozin, Zenaïde. *Odysseus: The Hero of Ithaca*. New York: Charles Scribner's Sons, 1898.

Burt and Ragozin present a smooth flowing, simplified version of the *Odyssey* which is fairly close to the original although the journey of Telemachus is postponed until late in the book. The use of archaic words such as *thee* and *dost* might disturb an inexperienced reader. While interesting, the few illustrations are only loosely connected with the text--as are some of the names in the glossary. An introductory section summarizes the events leading up to the fall of Troy.   6+

36.   Carpenter, Edmund Janes. *Hellenic Tales: A Book of Golden Hours with the Old Story-Tellers*. Boston: Little, Brown, and Company, 1923 (originally published in 1906).

This book consists of adaptations of myths drawn from many ancient sources, including Apollodorus, Ovid, Homer, Apuleius, Moschus, Bacchylides, and Vergil. Carpenter follows his ancient sources closely and lists them below the titles of the stories in the table of contents. He writes in a very smooth flowing style, both simplifying with a view to bowdlerization and adding descriptive details. Occasionally, a passage (in translation) is quoted. There are no illustrations in this book. This book was also published under the title *Long Ago in Greece: A Book of Golden Hours with the Old Story-tellers* (Boston: Little, Brown, and Company, 1906).   6+

37.   Carpenter, Edmund Janes. *Long Ago in Greece: A Book of Golden Hours with the Old Story-tellers* (Boston: Little, Brown, and Company, 1906) (see preceding entry).

38.   Carpenter, Frances. *Wonder Tales of Horses and Heroes.* Illustrated
        by William D. Hayes. Garden City, New York: Doubleday and
        Company, Inc., 1952.

        In this collection of stories from around the world, Greece is
        represented by the chapter entitled "The Flying Horse, Pegasus."
        Carpenter retells the myth of Bellerophon and Pegasus, weaving in the
        story of Medusa. She embellishes the material found in the ancient
        sources, changing a few details. She writes as a narrator/teacher. A
        large line drawing of Bellerophon riding Pegasus precedes the
        story.   5+

39.   Carpenter, Frances. *Wonder Tales of Seas and Ships.* Illustrated by
        Peter Spier. Garden City, New York: Doubleday and Company, Inc.,
        1959.

        Greece is represented in this collection of sea tales from around the
        world. The chapter entitled "Pelops and Poseidon" concerns a father
        and son watching a play about how with Poseidon's assistance Pelops
        defeated Oenomaus in a chariot race. The myth on which the drama
        was based follows. In retelling it, Carpenter combines material from
        various ancient sources. She creates a fair amount of dialogue and
        many descriptive details. There is large line drawing at the beginning
        of the chapter on Pelops.   6+

40.   Cather, Katherine Dunlap. *Pan and His Pipes and Other Tales For
        Children.* Foreword by Francis Elliott Clark. Camden, New Jersey:
        Victor Talking Machine Company, 1916.

        This book is of antiquarian as well as literary interest; for at the end of
        each chapter, Cather lists the titles of Victor Records that pertain to the
        chapter. The Victrola is mentioned in the "Foreword," which concerns
        children and music. Each of the ten chapters of the book is a story
        related to music. These include "The Violin Makers of Cremona,"
        "The Holy Grail," and "The Songs of Hiawatha." In the first chapter,
        "Pan and His Pipes," Cather introduces Pan and reveals how he came
        to make the first Syrinx, or Pan Pipe. In the second chapter, "The
        Tortoise That Gave the World Music," she relates how Mercury made
        the first lyre and why Midas' ears were turned into ass' ears. Though
        she does not mention her ancient sources, she follows them closely
        enough for the classicist to recognize that they are the *Homeric Hymns*
        and Ovid's *Metamorphoses.* One of the illustrations (all of which are

black and white) shows Pan playing his pipes; another shows Apollo playing his lyre; a third is of Apollo and the Muses. The first letter of each chapter is illuminated. Small print allows much information to be included in this diminutive book.   6 +

41.   Chadwick, Mara Louise Pratt (see Pratt-Chadwick, Mara Louise).

42.   Chaundler, Christine. *A Year Book of the Stars*. Illustrated by Tom Godfrey. London: A. R. Mowbray and Company, Limited, 1956.

After quoting "Twinkle, Twinkle, Little Star," Chaundler, in her first chapter, discusses the history of astrology, the signs of the zodiac, and the difference between stars and planets. In the twelve succeeding chapters, she briefly retells the numerous classical myths associated with each month. She also includes some astronomical information. Chaundler never mentions her sources; however, all the Greek and Roman myths she relates are simplified versions of material found in ancient works. The last section of the final chapter, an essay on the Star of Bethlehem, reflects the writer's Christian beliefs. Captions describe the action depicted in the carefully detailed line drawings. At the beginning of the book are a rhyme on the signs of the zodiac and a zodiacal calendar.   6 +

43.   *Childcraft: Stories of Fact and Fancy*. Volume Two. Chicago: W. F. Quarrie and Company, 1937.

The "Myths and Legends" section of this anthology of children's literature contains five stories from ancient Greek and Roman mythology. Three--"Pandora," "The Miraculous Pitcher," and "The Golden Fleece"--are simplified versions of Nathaniel Hawthorne's retellings (see Hawthorne, *A Wonder Book*). Two--"Persephone" and "Phaëthon"--are selections from Flora J. Cooke's *Nature Myths and Stories for Little Children* (see below). Each of the carefully detailed illustrations (some in color) is inset in the text immediately after the passage that describes the action shown in it.   4 +

44.   Church, Alfred J. *The Aeneid for Boys and Girls*. New York: The
        Macmillan Company, 1922 (originally published in 1908).

        Though he stays quite close to the wording of the *Aeneid*, Church
        presents the events in chronological order. As a result, Aeneas is first
        introduced in Chapter 2; and Carthage is first mentioned in Chapter 7.
        As might be expected in a children's version, the love story of Dido
        and Aeneas is downplayed. Dido's curse is not included, but her death
        on the funeral pyre is briefly described. The final chapters of Church's
        book give a short history of Rome up to the invasion of Britain. This
        book, originally published in 1908, is a simplified version of Church's
        Stories from Virgil, which was written for the general public.   6 +

45.   Church, Alfred J. *The Iliad for Boys and Girls*. New York: The
        Macmillan Company, 1930 (originally published in 1907).

        Directed at 8 to 10 year-olds, this book presents the *Iliad* in simple
        language yet remains remarkably close to the original though Odysseus
        is called Ulysses. Some of the dialogue has an old-fashioned flavor,
        which, however, does not impede the reader's understanding. The
        introduction and final chapters concern the Trojan War. There are 16
        illustrations (a few in color). This book is a simplified version of
        Church's *The Story of the Iliad* (1892), which was intended for the
        general public.   6 +

46.   Church, Alfred J. *The Odyssey for Boys and Girls*. Illustrated with
        designs by John Flaxman. New York: The Macmillan Company, 1906
        (see next entry).

47.   Church, Alfred J. *The Odyssey of Homer*. Illustrated with designs by
        John Flaxman. New York: The Macmillan Company, 1951.

        Employing the narrative voice of the storyteller-teacher, Church relates
        the tales told in the *Odyssey*. The accounts of individual incidents
        follow Homer quite closely, including many small details; but the
        arrangement of the ancient work is not followed, and Odysseus'
        encounter with the Lotus Eaters is omitted. The illustrations are
        designs of John Flaxman which have been colorized. This book is a
        simplified version of *The Story of the Odyssey* (1892), which was
        intended for the general public. It was first published in 1906 under
        the title *The Odyssey for Boys and Girls*.   6 +

48.   Clark, I. E. *Pandora and the Magic Box.* 'Stage Magic' Plays:
        Schulenburg, Texas, 1968.

        This little play is based on Nathaniel Hawthorne's "The Paradise of
        Children" (see Hawthorne, *A Wonder Book*). The play book includes
        the script, production notes, detailed stage directions, and a page of
        photographs of the presentation of the play by junior-high-school
        students.   6+

49.   Clarke, Helen Archibald. *A Child's Guide to Mythology.* New York:
        The Baker and Taylor Company, 1910.

        In her prefatory note, Clarke states that her intention is to provide solid
        mythological knowledge and to present interesting stories "which will
        . . . almost unconsciously, lay a firm foundation for the fascinating
        study of Comparative Mythology" (p. 8). Clarke's first chapter (now
        naturally a bit dated) is a discussion in simple language of various
        theories of myth, ranging from that of Theognis to that of Sir James G.
        Frazer. Greek and Roman myths are scattered throughout the various
        chapters, which include "Animals in Cultural Myths"; "Tree and Plant
        Myths"; "Myths of the Sun, Moon, and Stars"; and "Mother-Myths and
        Child-Myths." All of the illustrations pertain to classical mythology.
        Clarke's main source for Greek and Roman myths is Charles Mills
        Gayley's *Classical Myths in English Literature,* which is based on
        Bulfinch's *Age of Fable* (See Bulfinch above). This book was later
        published under the title *A Guide to Mythology for Young
        Readers.*   6+

50.   Cole, Pamela McArthur. *Heroes of the Olden Time.* New York:
        Richardson, Smith and Company, 1904.

        Cole introduces the young reader to Hercules, Theseus, Jason,
        Meleager, Edipus [*sic*], and Perseus. She writes in uncomplicated
        sentences, indicates the pronunciation of a name the first time that it is
        mentioned, and explains difficult words. Her use of the Anglicized
        spellings may prove confusing to some. Only rarely does Cole deviate
        from story lines found in the ancient sources. Her elaborations are not
        misleading. Small line drawings, many of which are based on ancient
        works of art, are scattered throughout the text.   4+

51.   Cole, Pamela McArthur. *The Story of the Golden Apple*. New York: Richardson, Smith and Company, 1902.

The golden apple in the title is the golden apple that Discordia threw into the wedding feast of Peleus and Thetis, thus beginning the chain of events which resulted in the Trojan War. The first half of the book is a simplified but comprehensive account of the Trojan War. The latter half is, in reality, a paraphrase of most of the *Odyssey* (Telemachus' adventures abroad and the reunion of Odysseus and Laertes are omitted). In her introduction, Cole describes the physical make-up of the ancient book and introduces her reader to Homer and the *Iliad*. Oddly enough, the *Odyssey* is not mentioned. Writing as an omniscient narrator, Cole explains cultural differences and occasionally comments on the actions of the characters. She uses the Latin name Ulysses for Odysseus and the Latin names of the deities. The first time a name appears, its accentuation is indicated. Finely detailed line drawings, some captioned, are interspersed in the text.   5 +

52.   *A Coloring Book of Ancient Greece: With Illustrations of the Artists of Those Times*. Santa Barbara, California: Bellerophon Press, 1970.

This book features full-page drawings for coloring of mythological and domestic scenes. Each drawing is based on an ancient Greek work of art, which is cited along with its current location. At the bottom of every drawing is a legend (in bold-face type) that indicates the subject of the picture. Under this, on many pages, there is a brief commentary. The cover of the book is colored reproduction of a red-figure vase painting of Athena by the Andokides Painter.   3 +

53.   Colum, Padraic. *The Adventures of Odysseus and the Tale of Troy*. Illustrated by Willy Pogány. New York: The Macmillan Company, 1918.

Though Colum never mentions either the *Iliad* or the *Odyssey*, his book is a combined and simplified version of the two epics of Homer. Dialogue as well as action is immediately recognizable to the classicist. In order to weave background material into the framework of the *Odyssey*, Colum takes the liberty of having Phemius (who sings of past events) accompany Telemachus on his voyage. Menelaus and Helen tell Telmachus all about Achilles (including the whole plot of the *Iliad*). The many illustrations, some of which are in color, serve both to beautify and to inform. This book was reprinted in 1925 and 1962 under the title *The Children's Homer: The Adventures of Odysseus and the Tale of Troy.*   6+

54.   Colum, Padraic. *The Children's Homer: The Adventures of Odysseus and the Tale of Troy.* Illustrated by Willy Pogány. New York: The Macmillan Company, 1962 (see preceding entry).

55.   Colum, Padraic. *The Golden Fleece and the Heroes Who Lived Before Achilles.* Illustrated by Willy Pogány. New York: The Macmillan Company, 1921.

Into his retelling of the story of Jason and the Argonauts, Colum weaves many additional myths, including those of Pandora, Demeter, Perseus, and Theseus. The attractive line drawings which illustrate the text are appropriately placed and immediately comprehensible. In some parts of this book, Colum follows the *Argonautica* of Apollonius Rhodius so closely that even speeches are recognizable. In other parts, he exercises great creative license. For example, the Argo forbids the Argonauts to enter the harbour of Pegasae on their return home. Having gone with Jason directly to Corinth, Medea uses a car drawn by dragons to fly alone to and from Iolcus, where she kills Pelias (in the manner described by Apollodorus).   6+

56.   Connolly, Peter. *The Legend of Odysseus.* Oxford: Oxford University Press, 1986.

In this coffee-table book, which invites browsing as well as reading, Connolly retells the story of the Trojan War as revealed in ancient works of literature. He also examines the legend from an archaeological point of view, adding a section on archaeological discoveries at the end of each chapter of his narrative. Site reconstructions, maps, and photographs provide insights into archaeology while captioned colored drawings show literary scenes. Connolly mentions only the *Iliad* and *Odyssey*, but in his adaptation of the story of the Trojan War, he draws from other ancient sources in addition to Homer.   6+

57.   Cooke, Flora Juliette. *Nature Myths and Stories for Little Children*. Chicago: A. Flanagan Company, 1895.

Cooke includes many stories based on classical myths. Some follow an ancient work quite closely; others are drastically different from all ancient versions. The stories are 3-4 pages in length and intended for use in grades 1-3. The illustrations are small but lovely, and an ornate letter decorates the beginning of each selection.   1-3

58.   Coolidge, Olivia E. *Greek Myths*. Illustrated by Edouard Sandoz. Boston: Houghton Mifflin, Company, 1949.

Blending material from various ancient sources (which are never mentioned), Coolidge tells each story in her own words. She creates narrative details and conversations as well as providing explanatory details. Coolidge is especially adept at retelling the seamier parts of the myths in such a way as to give accurate information without offending or shocking. This book is divided into seven sections: "Stories of the Gods," "Loves of the Gods," "Early History of Mankind," "Man's Rivalry with the Gods," "Love Stories of the Heroes," "Adventure Stories," and "Great Heroes." In her introduction, Coolidge comments on each of the major deities. She also briefly discusses the development of myth and notes that knowledge of the Greek myths is essential to the understanding of much of western literature.

Eye-catching, carefully detailed line drawings are coordinated with the text. The book features a table in which the chief functions and symbols of deities are listed as well as a guide to the pronunciation of names.   6 +

59.   Coolidge, Olivia E. *Hercules and Other Tales from Greek Myths*. Illustrated by David Lockhart. New York: Scholastic Book Services, 1967.

This paperback contains abridged versions of stories from *Greek Myths* by Olivia Coolidge (see above). The name Heracles was changed to Hercules. Subjects other than Hercules include Arachne, Philemon, Pygmalion, Demeter, Icarus, Atalanta, and Theseus. Eye-catching black on beige illustrations show characters in critical moments of action.   6 +

60.   Coolidge, Olivia E. *The Trojan War*. Illustrated by Edouard Sandoz. Boston: Houghton Mifflin Company, 1952.

Employing a style (very smooth flowing) and tone similar to that found in modern historical romances, Coolidge tells the story of the Trojan War from the wedding of Peleus and Thetis to the reunion of Odysseus and Penelope.   Though many conversations and descriptive details come out of Coolidge's imagination, they are consistent with traditional accounts.   Myths, for example, that of Oenone, which were recorded by later writers, are included as well as those treated of by Homer and the Greek tragedians.   All of the striking black and beige illustrations show scenes of action.   At the beginning of the book there is a list of the chief characters on each side of the conflict.   At the end, there is a list of characters and places, which includes a pronunciation guide.   6 +

61.   Cornell, James. *Mythical Monsters*.   New York: Scholastic Book Services, 1973.

Descriptions of mythical monsters from around the world may be found in this little book.   The physical appearance of each creature, its habitat, and its habits are indicated.   Monsters are listed in alphabetical order, and descriptions are no more than a page in length.   Little known monsters, such as the Ethiopian Leucrotta, which is mentioned in the works of Pliny the Elder, as well as famous monsters, such as the Chimaera are included.   A full-page, cartoon-like drawing accompanies each entry.   In one corner of the illustration is the name of the monster with its pronunciation in parentheses after it.   The introduction of the book discusses how mythical monsters may have originated.   Suggestions as to the origin of a specific creature are worked into the commentary on that creature.   Only one inaccuracy was detected: the text says that one of the Hydra's heads was human.   4 +

62.   Couzens, Reginald C. *The Stories of the Months and Days*.   New York: Frederick A. Stokes Company, 1923.

This book contains a treasure trove of calendarial information. Featuring a smoothly flowing text, it may be read from cover to cover or used as a reference book.   In his introduction, Couzens discusses the divisions of time, including an explanation of the Julian and Gregorian calendars.   He devotes one chapter to each of the months of the year and one to each of the days of the week. Individual chapters begin with an explanation of the name of the month or day. Pertinent Roman and/or Nordic mythological and historical material comes next, followed by comments on modern (British) customs which grew out of ancient practices. The penultimate chapter of the book treats of the meaning of myth (with emphasis on solar interpretations). The last chapter consists of notes on special days such as the Sabbath and Maundy Thursday. Interspersed throughout the text are black and white reproductions of famous paintings and statuary and quotations from English literature (Some of the literary passages might prove a bit difficult for students at the junior high level).   6 +

63.   Cox, George William. *A Manual of Mythology in the Form of Question and Answer*. New York: Leypoldt and Holt, 1868.

This fascinating book, as its title indicates, consists of questions and answers about mythology--about ninety per cent of which pertains to classical mythology. The author frequently draws on his knowledge of comparative mythology and on the solar theory of Max Müller. He rarely mentions primary sources other than Homer, but the advertisement at the beginning of this book does cite contemporary scholars to whom Cox is indebted. Though this book was intended to serve as a student's manual of mythology, today it is primarily of interest to teachers of classical mythology. The book contains only a few small illustrations.   8 +

64.   Cox, Miriam. *The Magic and the Sword: The Greek Myths Retold*. Illustrated by Harold Price. Evanston, Illinois: Row, Peterson and Company, 1960.

According to the introduction, the purpose of this book is to introduce children to classical mythology by the retelling of the myths as stories to be read for entertainment. The text is divided into three sections: "When the World Was New," "Gods and Heroes," and "Troy and the Long Voyage." Individual chapters are quite short and may be read independently as well as in sequence. At the end of most chapters are etymological comments. Even though the myths are related in simple language and greatly abridged, Cox remains close enough to the original works in content and tone for the classicist to identify the ancient sources. Features of the book include numerous illustrations (black and white), a map, and an annotated index with a pronunciation guide.   Pronunciation is also indicated the first time that a name appears in the text.   4+

65.   Crawford, John Raymond. *Greek Tales for Tiny Tots*. Illustrated by Pauline Avery Crawford.   Bloomington, Illinois: Public School Publishing Company, 1929.

In a witty, colloquial manner, Crawford introduces various mythological characters, ranging from Bacchus in "The Boy Who Drank Goat's Milk" to Camilla in "The Girl Who Was Thrown on a Spear." Crawford retells myths freely, adding superfluous and often anachronistic details; for example, after Perseus marries Andromeda, he gives her "a five pound box of chocolates every morning for breakfast" (p. 46). The selections, each two pages in length, are written to be read to rather than by small children. A black and white comic strip, subtitled with very basic sentences, summarizes each story. The author includes a pronunciation guide.   4+

66.   Crowell, Robert L. *The Lore and Legends of Flowers*. Illustrated by Anne Ophelia Dowden.   New York: Thomas Y. Crowell, 1982.

This coffee-table-type book, which has large colored illustrations of flowers, provides intriguing information about the history, lore, and uses of ten familiar flowers. The chapter on the narcissus gives the account of the origin of the narcissus found in the *Homeric Hymn to Demeter* (Crowell incorrectly attributes the version to Hesiod) and also that found in Ovid. The chapter on roses mentions that they were associated with the Roman goddess Venus as well as the Greek god Dionysus. Throughout the book, there are references to flowers in Greek and Roman culture. The book contains a relatively thorough index.   7+

67.   Cruse, Amy. *The Book of Epic Heroes*. London: G. G. Harrap and Company, Limited, 1927 (see next entry).

68.   Cruse, Amy. *The Young Folk's Book of Epic Heroes*. Boston: Little, Brown, and Company, 1927.

This book offers condensed versions of epic poems from around the world. The introduction explains what epic poetry is and discusses the changes in the concept of hero throughout the ages. Classical epic is represented by a condensation of the *Odyssey*. After a quick summary of the Trojan War, Cruse relates, in chronological order, the adventures of Odysseus from his departure from Troy to his reunion with Penelope, who, in this version, recognizes her husband as soon as she sees him waiting to greet her. In addition to the above change, Cruse alters just a few details. She only refers to Telemachus' journey and Odysseus' visit to the Underworld. Several captioned illustrations (only one of which is colored) accompany the text. The London edition of this book has the title *The Book of Epic Heroes*.   6 +

69.   Cruse, Amy. *The Young Folk's Book of Myths*.   Boston: Little, Brown, and Company, 1937.

The first quarter of this book of myths from around the world treats of classical mythology. In addition to the myths of Arachne, Persephone, Phaeton [*sic*], and Orpheus, there are chapters on Prometheus, Hermes, and Hercules. In her retellings, Cruse blends material from various ancient sources, adding a wealth of descriptive detail and some dialogue. Features of the book include a preface addressed to children, in which the author discusses the development of mythology in primitive culture, and a pronunciation guide. The main illustrations, some of which are in color, are reproductions of famous works of art (with title and artist indicated).   7 +

70.   Daly, Kathleen N.   *Greek and Roman Mythology A to Z: A Young Reader's Companion*. Illustrated with photographs researched by Elyse Rieder. New York: Facts on File, Inc., 1992.

The entries in this coffee-table mini-encyclopedia include not only mythological figures but also works of literature, for example, "*The Iliad*"; major authors, for example, "Euripides"; and important places, for example, "Magna Graecia." The extensively cross-referenced entries are brief, but many contain references to works of art and literature, both ancient and modern, as well as commentary (generally historical). The vocabulary is quite sophisticated. Some inaccuracies occur. For example, Daly relates that Phaëthon was turned into a swan (p. 97). In Ovid's *Metamorphoses*, which she notes is the most complete source of the story, a relative of Phaëthon is turned into a swan. In her entry on Pygmalion (p. 102), Daly again cites Ovid but gives a late and little-known version of the story. On p. 88, Zeus is identified as god of light. Perhaps Daly is extending the signification of his name, "Bright Sky."

In her long introduction, Daly comments on the origin of mythology and discusses various aspects of Greek and Roman culture. She designed the section entitled "How to Use This Book," to give a general survey of Greek mythology. At times, especially in the introduction, Daly's generalizations are misleading. For example, she notes that the ancient Greeks believed that their deities were originally human beings (p. iv). This was the belief of Euhemerus but not of all the ancient Greeks.

Daly includes a map of the ancient Greek world, a bibliography of secondary sources (adult level), and a thorough index. Most of the illustrations are photographs of works of art. Each has a full-sentence legend.   7+

71.   D'Aulaire, Ingri and D'Aulaire, Edgar Parin. Illustrated by Ingri and Edgar Parin D'Aulaire. *Book of Greek Myths*. Garden City: Doubleday and Company, 1962.

This book provides an excellent overview of classical mythology. After preliminary comments on the nature of the Greek deities, the D'Aulaires turn their attention to the pre-Olympian deities, then to Zeus and his family, next to minor gods and woodland creatures, and finally to mortal descendants of Zeus. In relating the stories associated with a character, the authors present material from ancient sources, which they simplify without much distortion. The text of the book is organized in such a fashion that although it is a continuing narrative, it may be read in part or used as a reference book (There is an annotated index and a mythological map).   Filled with colored illustrations, this book is attractive enough to serve as a coffee-table book.   6+

72.   Davidson, Josephine. *Teaching and Dramatizing Greek Myths*. Illustrated by Fiona Starr. Englewood, Colorado: Teacher Ideas Press, 1989.

This book was designed as a text for introducing junior high school students to Greek mythology through either puppet performances or student dramatization. Using E. V. Rieu's translation of the *Odyssey* and many secondary sources, which she lists in her bibliography,

Davidson wrote the thirteen dramas which she presents in this book. For eight of the plays, she includes teachers' notes, vocabularies, transparency masters, activities, tests, games, and puzzles. At the end of the book are found 1) suggestions for general activities, for example, a star project; 2) production notes for puppet plays; 3) a chart of deities (in which she unfortunately characterizes Zeus as stupid); and 4) answer keys. Line drawings show characters in the text. 5 +

73. Davies, Anthea. *A White Horse With Wings*. Illustrated by Brigitte Bryan. New York: The Macmillan Company, 1968.

Two of the five stories in this book are based on classical myths. Davies creates her own version of the story of Pegasus and Bellerophon. In it, the task of killing the Chimaera is assigned to Bellerophon to prevent him from marrying the king's daughter. He throws away the magic bridle which the king gives him, choosing to ride Pegasus bareback after killing the Chimaera. He marries a farm girl, who teaches him to milk cows. Much of the Davies' version is devoted to the description of equestrian maneuvers. In "Alcestis," Davies remains a little closer to the accounts found in ancient sources but still makes major changes in both the plot line and the tone. 5 +

74. Deblander, Gabriel. *The Fall of Icarus*. Paris-Gembloux: Duculot, 1978.

Part of The Children's Art Series, *The Fall of Icarus* is based on Pieter Brueghel's painting of the same name. The painting appears as the frontispiece and on the cover of the book. Relevant sections of it serve as illustrations throughout. Deblander imagines what each character in the painting is saying. Following Ovid's account, he also relates the events leading up to the death of Icarus. Just as there are anachronisms in the painting, so there are in the text, for example, mention of a galleon sailing to Mexico. At the end of the book is a short essay which presents the myth of Daedalus and Icarus and describes Brueghel's painting in detail. 5 +

75.   Dempsey, Michael W., editor-in-chief. *Greek Myths and Legends.*
        Macdonald Junior Reference Library. London: B.P.C. Publishing
        Limited, 1968.

        Most of this book consists of a dictionary of classical mythology. The
        entries, arranged in alphabetical order and cross-referenced, range from
        Achilles to Pelias to Zeus. They encompass most of the best known
        Greek myths. The opening chapters of the book concern creation and
        the reigns of Uranus, Cronus, and Zeus. As a result of the attempt to
        simplify and condense, some statements are misleading. An editor's
        note states that, in the case of multiple versions, "the most commonly
        accepted story has usually been chosen" (p. 8). Notable are two
        exceptions: 1) Epimetheus opens Pandora's box; 2) Oedipus blinds
        himself with his sword. Nestor's father, Neleus, is called Noleus on
        p. 52. Richly colored illustrations make up a good portion of the book.
        The book contains a map of the ancient Greek world, a list of the
        Roman equivalents of the Greek deities, a gazetteer of ancient Greece,
        an index, and a list of metric equivalents.   6+

76.   De Sélincourt, Aubrey. *Odysseus the Wanderer.* Illustrated by
        Norman Meredith. New York: Criterion Books, 1956.

        In a note at the end of his book, De Sélincourt states that his objective
        was to whet the appetites of his young readers for the *Odyssey*. His
        book is really a biography of Odysseus, supposedly related by a
        modern Greek narrator (who cannot resist inserting his own comments
        and aphorism upon aphorism into his tale). De Sélincourt allows his
        imagination to run free, preserving or changing traditional accounts as
        he pleases. For example, he has the narrator say that in order to avoid
        joining the expedition against Troy, Odysseus "would have feigned
        sickness, feigned madness," (p. 38), which he actually did in the
        ancient version of the story (cf. Hyginus, *Fabulae* 95). On the other
        hand, in relating the Cyclops incident, De Sélincourt follows the
        Odyssey quite closely. Numerous line drawings, placed at appropriate
        places in the text, make important scenes more memorable.   4+

77.   Dolch, Edward W.; Dolch, Marguerite P.; and Jackson, Beulah F.
        Greek Stories for Pleasure Reading. Illustrated by Marguerite Dolch
        and Robert S. Kerr. Champaign: Garrard Publishing Company, 1955.

        Most of the stories in this book concern the adventures of Greek
        heroes. The book is part of a series designed for children who have

some reading difficulties. The myths are rewritten in simple language, using "The First Thousand Words for Children's Reading," a basic vocabulary list compiled by E. W. Dolch, a professor of education. The ancient Greek concepts of deity and hero are introduced in the "Foreword." The stories contain a large amount of fabricated conversation. There are a few inaccuracies, resulting primarily from the simplification process; for example, Theseus fights the Spider. Medea is spelled Media in the story of Theseus but Medea in the story of Jason and in the pronunciation guide at the back of the book. Full-page illustrations show action scenes, which are described in the "List of Pictures." The use of various shades of purple to highlight causes the reader to pay more attention to the illustrations. 4 +

78.   Duthie, Alexander. *The Greek Mythology: A Reader's Handbook.* Westport, Connecticut: Greenwood Press, 1979 (see next entry).

79.   Duthie, Alexander. *The Greek Mythology for Schools.* Edinburgh: Oliver and Boyd, n.d.

In his preface, Duthie explains his methodology: "The object of the present little book is to provide in *connected* form enough information to cover all the ordinary allusions met with, so that by reading it through, the student may get a conspectus of the whole field; while, by means of a copious index, it may also fulfill the function of the Classical Dictionary" (n.p.). Features of this book include a map of ancient Greece, captioned line drawings, an explanation of the variations in mythological names, a discussion of methods of interpreting myths, and three genealogical charts ("The Trojan House," "The Theban House," and "The Race of Tantalus"). Since this book is written for a mature reader, most grammar school students would probably find it somewhat difficult. This book was subsequently published with the title *The Greek Mythology: A Reader's Handbook,* first by Oliver and Boyd (1932) and then by Greenwood Press (1979). 8 +

80.   Edmondson, Elizabeth. *The Trojan War.* Illustrated by Harry Clow. New York: New Discovery Books, Macmillan Publishing Company, 1992.

Part of the Great Battles and Sieges series, this coffee-table book presents both archaeological and mythological information about the

Trojan War. Edmondson begins with the question "Fact or Fiction?" and concludes by saying "The discovery of Troy by archaeologists does not mean that there *was* a war such as Homer describes" (p. 29). She gives historical commentary, then discusses all of the major characters in the Trojan War saga. Next, she tells what happened between the failure of Eris to receive an invitation to the wedding of Peleus and Thetis and Athena's punishment of the Greeks for dragging Cassandra away from her statue. On the final page of her narrative, Edmondson summarizes the post-war lives of Odysseus, Agamemnon, Menelaus, and Aeneas. She also comments on the historicity of the story. Though Edmondson mentions only Homer, she gleans material from other ancient sources. Calchas is spelled Calches (p.18), and Phthia is spelled Phithia (p. 19). The book contains a glossary of words in bold print in the text, including "allies," "Nereid," and "scholar." Edmondson also provides a map of Mycenaean-age kingdoms, an index, and suggestions for further reading--mostly historical. Some pages of the text are superimposed on full-page colored illustrations. Others have a combination of colored and black and white illustrations, some of which are photographs.   6+

81.   Elgin, Kathleen. *The First Book of Mythology*. Illustrated by Kathleen Elgin. New York: Franklin Watts, Inc., 1955.

In this excellent little book, Elgin manages to cover most of the major myths with only a few changes of detail. She begins with a chapter on how myth developed. Elgin includes a pronunciation guide and a list of important deities as well as colorful, monothematic illustrations.   4+

82.   Espeland, Pamela. *The Story of Arachne*. Illustrated by Susan Kennedy. Minneapolis: Carolrhoda Books, Inc., 1980.

Espeland presents a simplified version of Ovid's account of Arachne. At the beginning of her book, Espeland provides an introduction to classical mythology and to Ovid. There is an error in the preface, for it states that Rome conquered Greece around 150 A.D. rather than 150 B.C. At the end of her retelling, Espeland adds a comment on the derivation of the English word *arachnid* and a pronunciation guide. Each of the many illustrations is done in shades of gray with one highlight color. Some of the characters in the illustrations have a medieval look to them; some, a modern look.   3+

83.   Espeland, Pamela. *The Story of Baucis and Philemon*. Illustrated by
        George Overlie. Minneapolis: Carolrhoda Books, Inc., 1981.

        Espeland incorporates much natural sounding dialogue with an
        American flavor into her retelling of Ovid's version of the myth of
        Baucis and Philemon. In her introduction, Espeland mentions Ovid's
        work and explains what a metamorphosis is. She also provides an
        introduction to classical civilization. A map compares ancient and
        modern Greece. Throughout the book, salient parts of the myths are
        shown in line drawings. On the last page is a pronunciation
        guide. 4+

84.   Espeland, Pamela. *The Story of Cadmus*. Illustrated by Reg Sandland.
        Minneapolis: Carolrhoda Books, Inc., 1980.

        Employing basic vocabulary words and short, easily readable sentences,
        Espeland tells the story of how Cadmus came to found Thebes. She
        includes his search for Europa, his visit to the oracle of Delphi
        (described as a spirit), his slaying of the dragon, and his building of
        Thebes with the aid of the Spartoi. Before launching into her story,
        Espeland introduces her reader to ancient Greek culture in general and
        to the House of Thebes in particular. At the end of her story, Espeland
        mentions the ruins of Thebes. She adds dialogue and descriptive detail
        to material found in the ancient sources, to which she remains faithful.
        Large line drawings, set in burnt-orange frames, tell the story visually.
        Features of the book include large print, a pronunciation guide, and a
        map of the ancient world. 4+

85.   Espeland, Pamela. *The Story of King Midas*. Illustrated by George
        Overlie. Minneapolis: Carolrhoda Books, Inc., 1980.

        In her preface, which provides a brief introduction to classical
        civilization, Espeland states that, according to Ovid's *Metamorphoses*,
        Midas underwent several changes but they did not benefit him. In
        subsequent chapters, Espeland retells the stories of Midas' golden touch
        and of his ass' ears. She embellishes Ovid's account with descriptions,
        explanations, and dialogue. She includes a pronunciation guide and a
        map that shows ancient Greece, Italy, and Phrygia. Copious black and
        white illustrations, highlighted in gold tones, portray both the actions
        and emotions of the characters. 4+

86.   Espeland, Pamela. *The Story of Pygmalion*. Illustrated by Catherine Cleary. Minneapolis: Carolrhoda Books, Inc., 1981.

Faithfully following Ovid's account, Espeland presents the story of Pygmalion, which she prefaces with brief remarks on ancient Greek and Roman civilization, on Ovid's *Metamorphoses*, and on George Bernard Shaw. This book features large print, short sentences, a pronunciation guide, and a map. The colored illustrations, which constitute a large part of the book, are most attractive. 4+

87.   Espeland, Pamela. *Theseus and the Road to Athens*. Illustrated by Reg Sandland. Minneapolis: Carolrhoda Books, Inc., 1981.

The book jacket blurb reveals that in preparing her version of the story of Theseus, Espeland consulted original Greek and Latin works but does not mention which ones. Espeland relates how Theseus came to be born in Troezen, why he chose to walk to Athens, and how he was recognized by Aegeus, whose wife, Medea had tried to kill her stepson. Theseus' encounters with various monstrous characters are described in detail. Using simple language, Espeland creates a large amount of dialogue and provides psychological insights as well as descriptive details. At the beginning of her narrative, she notes that the places mentioned were real places and includes a colored map showing them. She also comments briefly on Greek civilization. The large colored illustrations found throughout the book emphasize the emotional states of the characters. There is a pronunciation guide at the end of this large-print book. 4+

88.   Evans, Cheryl and Millard, Anne. *Greek Myths and Legends*. Illustrated by Rodney Matthews et al. London: Usborne Publishing, Limited, 1985.

Through the extensive use of cross-references, the authors pack a tremendous amount of material into this 64-page book. The main section of the text, entitled "Who's Who in the Greek Myths" and printed in small type, is really a mythological dictionary. The rest of the book consists of short discussions of various topics, such as the Trojan War. Creation myths and love stories are included. Major deities and heroes are treated of individually. Bold-faced print is used to indicate that a name may be found in the "Who's Who." There are maps of ancient Greece and Troy as well as commentary on ancient Greek history and culture. In the first chapter, which is addressed to the young reader, the authors give directions for using their book most effectively; they discourse on the meaning of myths; and they provide a list of major ancient Greek sources of myth. They state that if multiple versions of a myth exist, the best-known version is used. The authors are especially good at bowdlerizing in such a way that the original story line is not damaged; however, they use the terms *demi-god* and *demi-goddess* without defining them. There are a few minor inaccuracies, undoubtedly resulting from attempts at simplification. For example, Mother Earth (nowhere called Gaea) is not described as being a personification of earth, and in fact, is credited with creating earth (p. 58). Color is employed not only in many illustrations but also to highlight blocked sections of the text. 7+

89.   Evslin, Bernard. *The Adventures of Ulysses*. Illustrated by William Hunter. New York: Scholastic Inc., 1969.

Evslin rewrites Homer's *Odyssey* to his own liking. For example, at the land of the Lotus Eaters, Ulysses, after propping open his tired eyelids with splinters of wood, singlehandedly pushes his ships with his men on them into the sea. Evslin's account of Ulysses' encounter with Polyphemus does not agree either with Homer's or with the version he gives in his *The Cyclops* (see Evslin, *Monsters of Mythology*). The "Geneology [*sic*] of Gods and Goddesses" and the end note on derivatives also contain deviations from the accounts given in the ancient sources. A small finely detailed stylized illustration (black on a beige ground) follows each chapter heading, and there is a map of Ulysses' route. 8+

90.   Evslin, Bernard. *The Dolphin Rider and Other Greek Myths*. Illustrated by Jerry Contreras. New York: Scholastic Book Services, 1976.

Evslin freely retells eleven myths, including those of Arion, Cadmus, and Orpheus. Besides adding descriptive passages and dialogue, Evslin arbitrarily makes substantial changes in ancient plot lines. A few examples follow: 1) To prevent Hope from dying, Foreboding remains in Pandora's golden box; 2) Psyche's job after her marriage to Cupid is to undo mischief to a marriage done by meddling in-laws; and 3) Circe, whose story is conflated with that of Calypso, has many ex-husbands, whom she has turned into swine. In his "Afterword," Evslin relates that the Romans adopted the Greek deities and then gives a list of the Greek and Latin names of the deities as well as their functions. In this book, Phaëthon is spelled Phaeton. A small black and beige illustration of the main character precedes each story.   5 +

91.   Evslin, Bernard. *Gods, Demigods, and Demons: An Encyclopedia of Greek Mythology.* New York: Scholastic Books, Inc., 1975.

Since Evslin combines material found in various ancient sources without indicating them and especially since he often follows a less known version of a myth, for example, Antigone steals the body of Polyneices before she buries it (p. 12), this book is not as valuable as it might have been. In "Oedipus," Evslin says that an oracle told Oedipus that he was the cause of the plague at Thebes because he had murdered his father and married his mother (p. 158). According to Sophocles' *Oedipus the King*, the Delphic Oracle revealed that the plague had resulted from the fact that Laius' death was unavenged. Entries in this book range from "Abas" to "Judgment of Paris" to "Zeus." Evslin writes in a smooth-flowing manner, using his imagination to create narrative details. The pronunciation of a proper name in an entry heading is indicated in parentheses after the heading. There are a few typographical errors, for example, Colonnus for Colonus (p. 12) and Prosperina for Proserpina (p. 194), the correct pronunciation of which is given. Only the cover of this paperback is illustrated.   7 +

92.   Evslin, Bernard. *Hercules.* Illustrated by Jos. A. Smith. New York: William Morrow and Company, 1984.

Using information found in ancient sources merely as a base, Evslin writes his own version of the life of Hercules, whose name, he says, means "Earth's glory" (rather than "Hera's glory"). Evslin changes plot lines; for example, Hercules kills the Nemean Lion by thrusting his spear into the creature's eye (p. 31) rather than by choking it. He adds new characters, such as Copreus (Dung Man), who does unpleasant tasks for Eurystheus. Evslin even changes the characteristics of characters. In this book, Nessus is not a centaur but a horseman whom people call "the centaur" (p. 134), and Iole is a child who lives with Tyresias [*sic*]. Drawings shaded in gray show key scenes.   8 +

93.   Evslin, Bernard. *Monsters of Mythology*. 25 volumes. New York:
         Chelsea House Publishers, 1987.

Twenty-one volumes of this series are devoted to classical mythology,
two to Norse mythology, and two to Celtic mythology. Using (often
abusing is the better word) the characters of classical mythology, Evslin
creates new myths and rewrites existing ones. *Cerberus*, one of the
better volumes, presents an entirely new story about the Hadean hound.
Evslin arbitrarily changes plot lines as a few examples will indicate.
In *The Cyclopes*, Ulysses tries to stop his men from entering the cave
of the Cyclops Polyphemus. Confronted by Polyphemus, who is at
home, Odysseus volunteers to do corrective surgery to provide the
Cyclops with an additional eye and attractive facial features. When
Polyphemus agrees to the surgery, Ulysses gives him wine as an
anesthetic, then clunks him over the head with a mallet to render him
unconscious. In Homer's *Odyssey*, it is Odysseus who wishes to wait
for the absent owner of the cave and to receive gifts from him. After
getting Polyphemus drunk with wine, Odysseus, aided by his men,
blinds the Cyclops by twisting a hot stake into his eye. In *The
Minotaur*, Theseus faces the Minotaur in an arena crowded with
spectators. He defeats the Minotaur with a spool of thread which
magically spins a cocoon around the monster's body in order that
Theseus may kill it with a sharpened stick. Daedalus, having fallen in
love with Pasiphaë, makes himself a wooden bull so that he may court
her. In *The Hydra*, Zeus allows Hera to kill only twelve people a year.
Evslin adds both major and minor characters. He sometimes changes
the features of existing characters; for example, throughout the series
Hecate, not Celaeno, is queen of the Harpies, who live in the
Underworld. Iole is the daughter of Iris; Callirhoë is the daughter of
Castelos (not Oceanus). Students who take a classical mythology
course after reading this set of books are bound to be confused. The
illustrations are especially impressive because they are colored
reproductions of actual works of art; however, like the text, they are
a combination of classical and non-classical, ancient and modern, even
though their captions are lines from the text. It is unfortunate that
Evslin feels compelled to alter traditional material rather than merely
adding characters and plot lines not found in the ancient versions. The
titles pertaining to classical mythology are *Amycus*, *Anteus*, *The
Calydonian Boar*, *Cerberus*, *Chimaera*, *The Cyclopes*, *The Dragon of
Boeotia*, *The Furies*, *Geryon*, *Harpalyce*, *Hecate*, *The Hydra*, *Ladon*,
Medusa, *The Minotaur*, *The Nemean Lion*, *Procrustes*, *Scylla and
Charybdis*, *The Sirens*, *The Spear-birds*, and *The Sphinx*. 7+

94.   Evslin, Bernard; Evslin, Dorothy; and Hoopes, Ned. *The Greek Gods*.
         Illustrated by William Hunter. New York: Scholastic Book Services,
         1966.

         This book is divided into two major sections--"The Pantheon" and
         "Nature Myths." In the first section, the authors introduce each of the
         Olympian deities, offering at least one myth about each. They provide
         psychological insights not found (and often not even suggested) in
         ancient sources; for example, Persephone "knew that part of her power
         over him [Hades] was disdain, and so kept flouting and abusing him"
         (p. 27). There are a few inaccuracies; for example, both Oranos [*sic*]
         and Cronos are killed. In the second section, the authors retell several
         famous myths. They embellish imaginatively and greatly, stating, for
         example, that people believed Eurydice to be a sorceress (p. 79) and
         that Aphrodite was used as the model for the creation of Pandora
         (p. 61). At the end of the book are found an "Afterword," in which
         reasons for studying ancient Greek mythology are set forth; a
         discussion of various English words derived from Greek mythology;
         and a bibliography, which includes John Updike's novel *The Centaur*
         as well as standard reference books on ancient Greek mythology. No
         primary sources or translations of them are listed.   6+

95.   Evslin, Bernard; Evslin, Dorothy; and Hoopes, Ned. *Heroes and
         Monsters of Greek Myth*. Illustrated by William Hunter. New York:
         Scholastic Book Services, 1967.

         This book is divided into two sections. In the first part, entitled
         "Demigods" (one wonders what definition of *demigod* the authors
         accepted), are the myths of Perseus, Daedalus, Theseus, and Atalanta.
         In the second part, called "Fables," are the myths of Pygmalion and of
         Midas as Hawthorne (see Hawthorne, *A Wonder Book*) tells it. The
         authors elaborate greatly, adding psychological insights through
         invented dialogue. Sometimes the embellishment alters the story found
         in the ancient sources. For example, ancient writers mention that
         Atalanta wrestled with Peleus and had a child by Meleager. The
         authors of this book describe Atalanta wrestling with Meleager (not
         Peleus) and feeling the effects of his "magic" when their bodies come
         into contact. After the Calydonian Boar Hunt, Atalanta tells Meleager
         that she loves him but does not want to live in a castle or wear dresses
         (p. 84). The manner of Acrisius' death is changed. In the
         "Afterword," the authors say that in Greek mythology, good and evil
         are aspects of the same energy, which emanates from the gods. This
         statement needs further elaboration since its meaning is not clear. At

the end of the book there is an annotated list of Greek and Roman deities, a list of mythological derivatives, and "A Bibliography for Supplementary Reading" for adults.   No primary sources (or translations of primary sources) are given. A modernistic black and white illustration introduces each chapter.   6+

96.   Fadiman, Clifton. *The Adventures of Hercules*. Illustrated by Louis Glanzman. New York: Random House, 1960.

This "biography" of Hercules covers all of the major events in the hero's life.   Though no ancient sources are mentioned, from the closeness of the text to the ancient works the classicist will recognize Xenophon's "Choice of Heracles" (*Memorabilia* 2.1. 21-34), Euripides' *Alcestis* and his *Trachiniae* as the ancient sources of three chapters. Fadiman writes in a smooth-flowing style, skillfully bowdlerizing without altering the original plot line.   Black and white illustrations, highlighted in dusty rose which matches the chapter titles, portray Hercules in action.   6+

97.   Fadiman, Clifton. *The Voyages of Ulysses*. Illustrated by William M. Hutchinson. New York: Random House, 1959.

This is a short, simple retelling of the *Odyssey* which lays stress on what the various characters say. The illustrations, all done in black and green, are especially effective and have captions to insure understanding.   4+

98.   Fahs, Sophia Blanche Lyon and Spoerl, Dorothy T. *Beginnings: Earth, Sky, Life, Death*. Boston: Beacon Press, 1958.

Two chapters in this book of creation myths are from classical mythology: "Nyx, the Bird of Night, and Her Golden Egg" and "A Box Full of Troubles" (Pandora's box). Though the authors say that their ancient source is Hesiod (p. 114), the first part of the account of the creation of the universe which they give is not from Hesiod. Furthermore, their account of Pandora follows Hawthorne (see Hawthorne, *A Wonder Book*) more closely then Hesiod.   The pronunciation of names is indicated.   There are three line drawings of Pandora.   This book is a combination and revision of two earlier books--*Beginnings of Earth and Sky* and *Beginnings of Life and Death*. It is a Unitarian religious education textbook.   4+

99.   Farjeon, Eleanor. *Mighty Men from Achilles to Julius Caesar.*
         Illustrated by Hugh Chesterman. New York: D. Appleton and
         Company, 1930.

         In her preface, Farjeon states that she has included both basically
         legendary (Achilles, Hector, Aeneas, Ulysses, Romulus) and truly
         historical figures in her book and that she has made no attempt to
         separate fact from fiction. A chapter and a short, simple poem
         (immediately following the chapter) are devoted to each hero. These
         highlight a few significant events in the hero's life. Each chapter has
         one full-page, captioned line drawing. There is a pronunciation guide
         at the end of the book.   4+

100.   Farmer, Florence Virginia. *Nature Myths of Many Lands.* New York:
         American Book Company, 1910.

         This reader consists of nature stories from around the world. The
         classical myths about the origin of the cock, frog, partridge,
         grasshopper, laurel, and narcissus (the version in which Narcissus
         thinks that the reflection is his sister) are included. Farmer retells the
         myths in short, uncomplicated sentences and follows the ancient plot
         lines fairly closely. She does, however, refer to the deities as kings
         and queens. Greek names are used for some characters; Latin names,
         for others. Line drawings show scenes described in the text.   4+

101.   Farmer, Penelope. *Daedalus and Icarus.* Illustrated by Chris Connor.
         New York: Harcourt Brace Jovanovich, Inc., 1971.

         Farmer focuses on the part of Daedalus' life between his murdering of
         his nephew and the drowning of his son. She enhances material from
         ancient accounts, adding descriptive details and dialogue. She portrays
         Daedalus as an overly proud individual. The text of the book is
         superimposed on striking but somewhat ominous illustrations.   6+

102.   Farmer, Penelope. *The Serpent's Teeth.* Illustrated by Chris Connor.
         New York: Harcourt Brace Jovanovich, Inc., 1971.

         After describing how a white bull rose out of the sea and carried off
         Cadmus' sister, Europa, Farmer relates how Cadmus' search for his
         sister led to the foundation of Thebes. Farmer embellishes Ovid's
         account with descriptive passages and dialogue. In her version, the

serpent has three heads; Athene, not the Delphic oracle, orders Cadmus to follow a cow; and the cow stops to graze instead of lying down at the site of Thebes. Since a paragraph of text is set in the corner of each double-page, colored illustration, the art commands the reader's attention. 6 +

103. Farmer, Penelope. *The Story of Persephone*. Illustrated by Graham McCallum. New York: William Morrow and Company, 1973.

Slightly embellishing upon the ancient accounts, Farmer tells the story of Demeter's search for her daughter. She adds much descriptive detail. The modernistic illustrations which accompany the text are large and colorful but have a cold, almost frightening aspect to them. 6 +

104. Farrar, Frank Albert. *Old Greek Nature Stories*. London: G. G. Harrap and Company, 1910.

Farrar's copious collection stresses the relationship between classical myths and nature. In his introductory chapter, Farrar compares ancient and modern attitudes toward nature. He then introduces the major Greek deities, pointing out connections with natural phenomena. He devotes chapters to stories about rivers, animals, trees, stones, etc. True to his ancient sources, Farrar skillfully weaves succinct retellings of myths into his discussions of various aspects of nature. Many of the myths give the etiology of a particular species. In addition to a table of contents and index (which gives the pronunciation of the more difficult names), Farrar provides, at the beginning of each chapter, a list of subjects in the chapter. Black and white plates show pertinent masterpieces of painting and sculpture. 6 +

105. Firth, Emma M. *Stories of Old Greece*. Boston: D. C. Heath and Co., 1894.

Intended as a supplementary reader for the third grade, this book provides an introduction to ancient Greek mythology. In retelling the myths, the majority of which come from Ovid, Firth embellishes the ancient accounts with an abundance of descriptive detail and with explanatory comments. She makes some changes; for example, Eurydice is Orpheus' companion, not his wife, and love as well as hope remains in Pandora's box. Bowdlerization is obvious. Features of the book include an introductory chapter on ancient Greek culture, a pronunciation guide, and captioned line drawings of individual characters.   3+

106.   Fisher, Leonard Everett. *Cyclops*. Illustrated by Leonard Everett Fisher. New York: Holiday House, 1991.

After a one-page introduction to Homer and the *Odyssey* (overlaid on a map of Odysseus' route), Fisher notes that the Greeks returning from Troy had difficult journeys because they had dragged Cassandra from a temple.   Then he describes Odysseus' encounter with the Cyclops Polyphemus. Working from Lattimore's translation of the *Odyssey* and other secondary sources which he mentions at the beginning of the book, Fisher tells the story in his own way.   He carefully preserves the story line but recasts the dialogue a bit.   He makes one major change in the order of events: Polyphemus tells the other Cyclopes about "Noman" after Odysseus and his men have sailed away rather than while they are entrapped in Polyphemus' cave.   Effective use of light in the dark-toned illustrations makes them particularly dramatic.   4+

107.   Fisher, Leonard Everett. *Jason and the Golden Fleece*. Illustrated by Leonard Everett Fisher. New York: Holiday House, 1990.

This attractive picture book is an account of the adult life of Jason.   It begins with Jason's being assigned the task of obtaining the Golden Fleece and ends with his becoming a wanderer after the death of his children at Medea's hands.   Fisher avoids gory details when recounting murders.   He makes a few very minor changes in stories.   Hylas is pulled into a spring on Lemnos rather that at Cius, and Pelias is called the cousin rather than the half uncle of Jason.   Fisher lists his sources--all secondary--at the beginning of the book.   A portion of the large-print text is superimposed over part of each double-page dramatic colored illustration.   4+

108.   Fisher, Leonard Everett. *The Olympians: Great Gods and Goddesses of Ancient Greece*. Illustrated by Leonard Everett Fisher. New York: Holiday House, 1984.

The text of this book is superimposed upon richly colored illustrations that show the deities and the objects associated with them.   The book is as informative as it is attractive.   After a general introduction, Fisher treats of each of the twelve Olympians separately, devoting a paragraph of discussion to each. In addition, in chart form he indicates the functions, Roman name, parents, and symbols of each. At the beginning of the book, there is a list of the Olympians and their functions and a bibliography (for adults). At the end is a genealogical chart of four generations of descendants of Heaven and Earth. The genealogical chart is superimposed on a drawing of a tree.   3+

109.   Fisher, Leonard Everett. *Theseus and the Minotaur*. Illustrated by Leonard Everett Fisher. New York: Holiday House, 1988.

Fisher focuses on the main events in Theseus' life. Using information derived from several secondary sources (which are listed at the beginning of the book), he does not consistently follow any one ancient account of the life of the hero. Moreover, Fisher adds narrative details and dialogue. Dramatic illustrations, which feature very large-size figures are found on every page. The text is superimposed over the illustration on every other page. There is a map showing the route of Theseus' sea voyage.   4+

110.   Forbush, William Byron. *Myths and Legends of Greece and Rome*. Illustrated by Frederick Richardson. Chicago: The John C. Winston Company, 1928.

Forbush retells, in simplified and condensed form, myths which have influenced modern literature. At the end of each chapter are a list of literary references (including ancient sources) and quotations relevant to the myth discussed in the chapter. The author's purpose is to entice the young reader to read some of the literary masterpieces on which his stories are based. In retelling myths, Forbush generally follows accounts given by the ancients, but occasionally he prefers modern versions. For example, the chapters on Midas and on Baucis and Philemon are adaptations of Hawthorne (see Hawthorne, *A Wonder Book*). The book is divided into five sections: "Stories of the Beginning," "Stories of Gods and Men," "Animal Stories," "Stories of Love and Life," and "Hero Tales." Features of the book include a pronouncing dictionary, large print, and full-page captioned illustrations (some in color). There are two prefaces, one addressed to students of about the fifth grade level and the other to teachers.   5+

111.   Francillon, Robert Edward. *Gods and Heroes, or the Kingdom of Jupiter*. Boston: Ginn and Company, 1895.

About three fourths of Francillon's comprehensive book (285 pages) is informative and true to ancient sources. The book, however, is vitiated by alterations and additions found throughout the text. Following are a few of these: Titan (singular) is the eldest son of Terra; Ariadne, unwinding a ball of thread, makes her way into the Labyrinth and cuts the bonds on Theseus' hands; and Echo tells Narcissus that he is the most beautiful being in the world and shows him his reflection in a pool. Francillon breaks the third-person narrative to interpret, to comment (especially on the influence of ancient Greek and Roman mythology on modern life), and to moralize. There are no illustrations. 4+

112.   French, Marion N. *Myths and Legends of the Ages*. Illustrated by Bette Davis. New York: Hart Book Company, Inc., 1956.

Included in this book are twenty Greek myths, five Roman legends (those of Romulus, Regulus, Camillus, Cincinnatus, and Cornelia), and fifteen of Aesop's fables. Each chapter is a brief retelling of a well-known story. Even though French adds dialogue and descriptive detail, the ancient plot lines are carefully preserved. Quotations from the text appear under the colored illustrations, which are based on them. The book has large print. This is a revised edition of *A Treasury of the World's Great Myths and Legends for Boys and Girls* by Joanna and Leonard Strong (see below). 6+

113.   Frenkel, Emily. *Aeneas: Virgil's Epic Retold for Young Readers*. Illustrated by Simon Weller. Bristol: Bristol Classical Press, 1986.

Often echoing the tone and wording of the original work, Frenkel retells the story of Virgil's epic. She increases the amount of dialogue. Each book of the *Aeneid* is treated of in a separate chapter. Frenkel adds a prologue on Paris and an epilogue on the events between the death of Turnus, at which point the *Aeneid* ends, and the founding of Rome. She includes a glossary. Striking lithographs serve as illustrations. 7+

114.   Gale, Agnes Spofford Cook. *The Children's Odyssey*. Illustrated with half tone cuts from photographs by Karl Schwier. Bloomington, Illinois: Public-School Publishing Co., 1912.

With the purpose of staying very close to Homer's work, Gale, as if addressing a group of children, retells the story of the *Odyssey*. She includes all of the significant incidents and adds explanations when they are required.   Events are related in chronological order.   Gale interrupts her description of Odysseus' visit with the Phaeacians to tell of Penelope's situation and Telemachus' journey.   The first two chapters of this book provide an introduction to the major Olympians and to Homer while the next three cover events from the birth of Paris to the end of the Trojan War.   The book, which has large print and a pronunciation guide, is an enlarged edition of an earlier work called *The Story of Ulysses*.   The illustrations are half tone cuts taken from Karl Schwier's photographs of frescoes of Preller.   5+

115.   Gale, Agnes Spofford Cook. *The Story of Ulysses*. Bloomington, Illinois: Public-School Publishing Company, 1897 (see preceding entry).

116.   Galt, Thomas Franklin. *The Rise of the Thunderer*. Illustrated by John Mackey. New York: Thomas Y. Crowell Company, 1954.

Combining information from many ancient sources and creating some new material, Galt relates the story of the world from its creation to the release of Prometheus from his bonds.   He centers his book on each successive ruler's fear of being overthrown by his offspring.   Through the use of descriptive passages of the type found in modern romance novels, Galt lays more stress on the physical attraction between Uranus and Gaea and Cronus and Rhea than the ancient mythographers did.   Moreover, he elaborates on the quarrel between Zeus and Poseidon over Thetis, a theme only referred to in classical literature.   In his notes on each chapter (which seem to be addressed to adults rather than young readers), Galt discusses his sources and gives his reasons for following one account rather than another.   His index is especially thorough.   Line drawings are well coordinated with the text.   4+

117.   Garfield, Leon and Blishen, Edward. *The God Beneath the Sea: A Recreation of the Greek Legends*. Illustrated by Zevi Blum. New York: Pantheon Books, 1971.

The word *recreation* in the subtitle says it all. The authors change ancient accounts as they like. For example, they make Uranus one of seven original Titans (in Hesiod's *Theogony*, he is the father of the Titans) and say that he is killed by Cronus (in ancient versions, Uranus is a god and therefore immortal). Moreover, they claim, with no ancient authority, that Uranus made the earth his personal garden. The main subject of this mini-novel is the life of Hephaestus between his being thrown down from Mount Olympus by Hera and his return to Olympus after being thrown down a second time by Zeus. Many other myths, for example, that of Deucalion and Pyrrha, are woven into the story. Although this book is frequently included in lists of readings for grammar school students, it contains a few somewhat suggestive scenes, for example, the love-making of Zeus and Hera on the night when Hephaestus was conceived (p. 29) and the rape of both Themis and Mnemosyne by Zeus (p. 26). Moreover, several of the rather disquieting modernistic illustrations feature nude figures. At the beginning of the book, the authors provide an annotated list of principal characters.   8?

118.   Garfield, Leon and Blishen, Edward. *The Golden Shadow*. Illustrated by Charles Keeping. New York: Pantheon Books, 1973.

Though this mini-novel is often included in lists of readings for grammar schools students, because it contains a few suggestive illustrations and scenes, for example, a rather explicit description of the rape of Thetis (p. 155), as well as difficult vocabulary words, it is more suitable for older readers. The book focuses on a wandering minstrel who hopes to see and eventually does see (in the last chapter) one of the deities about whom he keeps hearing and whose stories he tells. This deity is Hermes, who, presumably, has come to lead the minstrel's soul to the underworld. Most of the book chronicles the life of Heracles. Many other myths, such as that of Atalanta and Melanion, are woven into the story. The authors preserve the main outlines of the myths given in ancient works but change some narrative details and add a wealth of others. The black and white illustrations are dramatic. Some might prove frightening to young children.   8?

119.   Gary, Charles L. *Flower Fables*. Illustrated by Carol Watson.
         McLean, Virginia: EPM Publications, Inc., 1978.

         Six of the twenty-eight stories about flowers pertain to characters in
         classical mythology. In retelling the myth of Hyacinthus and that of
         Persephone (in connection with the pomegranate), Gary follows the
         ancient accounts. In the relating the myth of Narcissus, he follows
         Ovid but bowdlerizes, stating that Narcissus thought that he saw the
         face of a nymph in the reflecting pond. In telling the stories of the
         rose, the iris, and the sunflower, Gary creates new myths involving the
         standard mythological figures. He builds each of his stories around a
         physical characteristic of the plant under discussion, for example, the
         thorn of the rose. The scientific name of the flower is given at the end
         of the selection. Great attention to detail in both the richly colored and
         the black and white illustrations causes the viewer to pause over
         them.   5+

120.   Gates, Doris. *A Fair Wind for Troy*.   Illustrated by Charles
         Mikolaycak. Viking Press, 1976.

         The main theme of this novelette, as reflected in its title, is the
         exchange of the life of Iphigenia for fair sailing winds. Woven into the
         plot are the stories of the oath of Helen's suitors, the judgment of
         Paris, the abduction of Helen and the refusal of Oenone to heal Paris.
         Thetis' attempts first to immortalize her son and then to keep him from
         going to war are described as well as Odysseus' feigning of insanity.
         The last chapter summarizes the events which occurred between the
         death of Iphigenia and the murder of Agamemnon. Using material
         from various ancient sources (never mentioned) as her basis, Gates
         gives every character a distinct personality. Each of the full-page,
         black and white drawings shows an important character. There is a
         pronouncing glossary at the end of the book. This book also comes in
         paperback (Puffin Books, 1984).   7+

121.   Gates, Doris. *The Golden God: Apollo*. Illustrated by Constantinos
         Coconis. New York: Viking Press, 1973.

         Arranging them in chronological order, Gates presents classical myths
         in which Apollo is a main character, for example, those of Daphne and
         Phaëthon. In many places her text actually reflects the tone and
         wording of the ancient source on which it is based. Gates adds a
         considerable amount of dialogue and descriptive detail but makes no

major alterations in retelling the stories. Her book features large print, arresting double-page, black and white illustrations; and a pronunciation key. Puffin Books published a paperback edition of this book in 1983.   4+

122.   Gates, Doris. *Heracles: Mightiest of Mortals*. Illustrated by Richard Cuffari. New York: Penguin Books, 1975.

Gates does an excellent job of blending myths about Heracles into a smooth-flowing biography which shows both the virtues and vices of the hero. She includes most of the stories about Heracles, the Alcestis myth being the most notable omission. The tales of Linus, Hylas, Antaeus, and Cacus are included. Gates follows the tradition that Heracles performed the twelve labours as expiation for the murder of his wife and son. Though she adds descriptive details and dialogue, Gates preserves the basic plot lines of her ancient sources. The glossary of this book indicates the pronunciation of proper names. Striking, double-page illustrations in beige and black show important moments in Heracles' life. There is a paperback edition of this book (Puffin Books, 1984).   6+

123.   Gates, Doris. *Lord of the Sky: Zeus*. Illustrated by Robert Handville. New York: Viking, 1972.

In addition to stories in which Zeus is a major character, this book contains the myths of Theseus, Daedalus, Midas, and Pentheus. For the most part, Gates follows the ancient sources, particularly Ovid, meticulously. She does, however, add a fair amount of descriptive detail and does, on occasion, change a few details. Hawthorne's (see Hawthorne, *A Wonder Book*) influence can be seen in her retelling of the Pandora myth. Pyrrha is spelled Pyrrah. The book has a glossary in which the pronunciation of proper names in indicated. Attractive ink drawings show action scenes described in the text. A paperback edition of this book appeared in 1982 (Penguin Books).   7+

124.   Gates, Doris. *Two Queens of Heaven*. Illustrated by Trina Schart Hyman. New York: Viking Press, 1974.

The queens of heaven to which the title refers are Aphrodite and Demeter. This book is primarily a collection of love stories, including that of Aphrodite and Anchises, which is rarely found in children's books. Following primary sources rather closely, Gates retells the stories in a straight-forward, non-suggestive manner, sometimes adding explanatory comments. The full-page line drawings are eye-catching, but some may object to those which feature topless goddesses, for example, that found on the cover of the book. There is a paperback version (Penguin Books, 1983), which has a more modest cover illustration.   6+

125.   Gates, Doris. *The Warrior Goddess: Athena.* Illustrated by Don Bolognese. New York: The Viking Press, 1972.

This collection of myths about Athena encompasses the stories of Arachne, Bellerophon, Perseus, and Jason.   Gates abridges and simplifies material from ancient sources. For greater vividness, she increases the proportion of dialogue. The book has large print and a pronunciation guide. Line drawings show action scenes. A paperback version of this book is available (Penguin Books, 1982).   4+

126.   Gerdes, Florence Marie, C. S. J. *The Aeneid: A Retelling for Young People.* Illustrated by George Ellen Holmgren. New York: St. Martin's Press, 1969.

This simplified version of the *Aeneid*, which includes all of the major episodes, retains the serious tone of the original work. In chapters 1-3, Gerdes relates in chronological order Aeneas' adventures from the fall of Troy to his arrival in Carthage. In chapters 4-12, she condenses and paraphrases the corresponding books of the *Aeneid*. Though she adds little elsewhere, she does have Aeneas think about the future as he watches Turnus die. Gerdes highlights the two invocations to the Muses (freely translated) by devoting a separate page to each. Pronunciation of names is indicated in the annotated list of proper nouns placed at the end of the book. The borders of the full-page, red, black, and beige illustrations feature ancient Greek patterns.   6+

127.   Gerstein, Mordicai. *Tales of Pan.* New York: Harper and Row, 1986.

Gerstein presents a biography of Pan, which includes his birth, his invention of panic, his love affairs, his musical contest with Apollo, his appearance at Marathon, and his death.   The book jacket lists Gerstein's sources as Ovid, Robert Graves' *The Greek Myths*, and Thelma Sargent's translation of the *Homeric Hymns*. Gerstein uses these sources as the basis of his account, but he elaborates much, particularly in telling the story of Iynx, Pan's daughter. The text of the book, especially the dialogue, is modern in tone, for example, "One kiss from me . . . and she'll forget that pea-brained oaf exists!" (p. 29). "Busy" line drawings, shaded in with watercolors, take up a large portion of each page.   6+

128.   Gibson, Michael. *Gods, Men and Monsters from the Greek Myths*. Illustrated by Giovanni Caselli. New York: Schocken Books, 1977.

This book encompasses the major Greek myths as well as many less popular ones, for example, the story of Apollo and Theophane. Most chapters focus on one mythological figure, but there are chapters on the House of Thebes and the fall of Troy. In his introductory chapter, Gibson discusses the geography of Greece, the reason for variant versions of myths, Homer, Schliemann, the attitude of the ancient Greeks toward their deities, and creation myths. In retelling the myths, Gibson combines material from a wide variety of ancient sources (with the exception of Homer, never mentioned in the text). He sometimes follows a lesser known version; for example, Haemon rescues and marries Antigone. Gibson adds a bit of dialogue and descriptive detail. He occasionally breaks his third-person narrative to involve his reader through the use of "we." There are a few serious inaccuracies; for example, Uranus fashions the earth, plants, and animals (p. 13); Zeus kills Cronus (p. 16); and Midas changes his children into gold (p. 128). This book has a colored map, a stylized genealogical chart, and an index. In addition to the copious illustrations (many in color) of scenes in the text, there is, at the beginning of each chapter, a line drawing which shows symbols associated with the character treated of in the chapter. These symbols are explained at the end of the book.   7+

129.   Gottlieb, Gerald. *The Adventures of Ulysses*. Illustrated by Steele Savage. New York: Random House, 1959.

This biography of Ulysses features many action scenes and gives Elpenor much more prominence than he has in the *Odyssey*. The author employs great license in changing details and creating dialogue. Odysseus' visit to the underworld is omitted as is his attempt to avoid the draft. Telegonus is not mentioned. The book ends with the aged Ulysses on the summit of Mount Neriton awaiting a peaceful death. Action-packed illustrations, a pronunciation glossary, an index, and a note on ancient Greek sources are provided.   6+

130.   Grammatky, Hardie. *Nikos and the Sea God*. Illustrated by Hardie
         Grammatky. New York: G. P. Putnam's Sons, 1963.

         Classical mythology and modern daily life on a small Greek island are
         nicely blended in this story of a young Greek boy's encounters with
         Poseidon. The book stresses Poseidon's ability to excite and calm the
         sea.   Appropriately, green-blue tones dominate in most of the
         illustrations, some of which are based on ancient works of art.   3 +

131.   Graves, Robert. *Greek Gods and Heroes*.   Illustrated by Dimitris
         Davis. Garden City, New York: Doubleday and Company, 1960.

         Centering each chapter on one character or set of characters, Graves
         presents condensed and simplified versions of the major Greek myths.
         He keeps the number of characters named to a minimum but includes
         many place names, preferring to use historical rather than mythological
         names, for example, Corfu instead of Scheria.   Graves sometimes
         conflates two very different ancient accounts into one story.   In his
         discussion of the Olympians, he stresses their unattractive traits and
         their indifference toward the human race.   While his introduction,
         which treats of the history of classical mythology, is basically factual,
         his conclusion is fanciful and allegorical: the Fates tell Zeus that his
         reign is over when the Emperor Julian is killed in 363 A.D.; then the
         Christians use the sign of the cross to drive out the deities who have
         moved from Mount Olympus to humble dwellings among the country
         people. The book has an index. Its monothematic illustrations, done
         in black, brown, and white, are comprehensible at a glance. This book
         was published in London in 1962 under the title *Myths of Ancient
         Greece.*   6 +

132.   Graves, Robert. *Myths of Ancient Greece*.   Illustrated by Joan
         Kiddell-Monroe. London: Cassell, 1962 (see preceding entry).

133.   Graves, Robert. *The Siege and Fall of Troy*. Illustrated by C. Walter
         Hodges. Garden City: Doubleday and Company, Inc., 1962.

         In his introduction, Graves calls his book "the first modern attempt to
         make the whole story from the foundation of Troy to the return of the
         victorious Greeks into a single short book for boys and girls" (p. 10).
         He also says that two thirds of his book is taken from ancient sources
         other than Homer but nowhere mentions the names of any of the

sources (They may be discovered by consulting Graves' adult mythology book, which is entitled *The Greek Myths*). Graves gives only one version of each myth, often preferring a little known one. He creates a few details, especially when bowdlerizing. This book features a map, a thorough index, and reddish brown illustrations, mostly of action scenes described in the text.   6 +

134.   *Great Myths and Legends: The 1984 Childcraft Annual.*   Chicago: World Book, Inc., 1984.

Three stories in this book--"The Sea Monster" (Perseus and Andromeda), "The Monster in the Maze" (Theseus and the Minotaur), and "The Many-Headed Monster" (Hercules and the Hydra)--are ancient Greek myths.   The myths are retold in simple language. Material from ancient sources (not mentioned) is embellished with description and dialogue.   Illustrations, some in color, show action scenes.   Each story in the book has its own introduction, which reveals the story's country of origin and provides background information. The introduction and an accompanying full-page black and white illustration are framed by a border featuring designs associated with the culture involved.   The book's preface delineates the characteristics of myths and legends.   At the end of the book is "A Short Dictionary of Myths and Legends," which includes characters not mentioned in the stories.   The pronunciation of each word is indicated, and a definition or description is provided.   Many entries, ranging from "Achilles" to "Muse" to "Styx" to "Zeus," pertain to ancient Greek mythology. Naiad is spelled Naid (p. 299).   6 +

135.   Green, Roger Lancelyn.   *A Book of Myths.*   Illustrated by Joan Kiddell-Monroe.   London: J. M. Dent and Sons, Ltd., 1965.

Seven chapters of this collection of myths of the ancient world and Scandinavia are devoted to classical mythology.   The prologue provides insights into the role of mythology in ancient Greek culture.   Each chapter is a conflation of mythical incidents derived from various ancient sources without preference necessarily being given to the most famous accounts.   Much of the dialogue is invented by Green.   Black line drawings, highlighted in blue or purple, show scenes from the text.   6 +

136. Green, Roger Lancelyn. *Heroes of Greece and Troy*. Illustrated by Heather Copley and Christopher Chamberlain. New York: Henry Z. Walck, 1961 (see Green, *Tales of the Greeks and Trojans*).

137. Green, Roger Lancelyn. *The Luck of Troy*. Illustrated by Margery Gill. London: The Bodley Head, Ltd., 1961.

The main character in this novel about the final months of the Trojan War is Nicostratus, the son of Helen and Menelaus, whom Helen took with her to Troy. Since ancient sources say very little about this character (Apollodorus and Hesiod mention him), Green creates most of his story. He makes Nicostratus a witness to the ransoming of Hector, the death of Achilles, and the stealing of the Palladion (the Luck of Troy). The novel ends with Nicostratus looking forward to returning to Greece after being rescued from death at the hands of Deiphobus. Green, who mentions his ancient authorities in the author's note at the end of the book, often chooses late and less familiar versions of myths for inclusion in his work. The book opens with an introduction to the characters and a prologue, in which Hermione describes the abduction of Helen by Paris. Most of the line drawings show Nicostratus. 7+

138. Green, Roger Lancelyn. *Mystery at Mycenae: An Adventure Story of Ancient Greece*. Illustrated by Margery Gill. New York: A. S. Barnes and Company, Inc., 1959.

The abduction of Helen by Theseus is the basis of this who-done-it for teenagers. The mystery has a twentieth-century tone though the subject is ancient. In a note at the end of the book, Green discusses his methodology, noting alterations of and additions to the traditional accounts. He includes a translation of his main source (Apollodorus, *Epitome* 1.23-24) and cites his other sources. Line drawings are interposed throughout the text. 7+

139. Green, Roger Lancelyn. *Old Greek Fairy Tales*. Illustrated by Ernest H. Shepard. London: Bell and Hyman, 1958.

Inspired by the version of the Perseus myth found in Lang's *The Blue Fairy Book* (see below), Green collects Greek myths with fairy-tale motifs. As he states in his preface, he rewrites the stories, eliminating as many names as possible and imitating the style in which fairy tales are told. The author's note at the end of the book is an apology addressed to those who would find fault with the free retellings. In it, Green lists all of his ancient sources and talks of the license which he takes in combining versions. Along with many famous tales, the lesser known myths of Rhodope, Polyidus, and Picus are found in this book.   6+

140.   Green, Roger Lancelyn. *Once Long Ago: Folk and Fairy Tales of the World*. Illustrated by Vojtiech Kubaista. London: Golden Pleasure Books, 1962.

The myth of Erysichthon and that of Atalanta (into whose story the myth of Meleager is woven) are included in this collection of folk tales from around the world.   Using Ovid as his primary source, Green retells the myths as folk tales, keeping names at a minimum. Erysichthon and Meleager are referred to as princes rather than by name; the Hamadryads are called Tree Fairies. The colorful mural-like illustrations bordering each page present a visual version of each story.   6+

141.   Green, Roger Lancelyn. *Stories of Ancient Greece*. Illustrated by Doreen Roberts. London: Paul Hamlyn, 1967.

This introduction to classical mythology contains a selection of different types of myths, including creation myths, love stories, and hero tales. In his prologue, Green gives a brief history of Greek literature and discusses the influence of Greek myths on modern literature.   The closeness of Green's text to its ancient sources varies from incident to incident.   Narrative passages often mirror the wording and tone of an ancient work; dialogue frequently stems from the author's imagination. The blending of earlier accounts and bowdlerizing occasionally result in flawed passages.   Large, richly colored illustrations entice the browser to read the text.   6+

142.   Green, Roger Lancelyn. *The Tale of Troy: Retold from Ancient Sources*. Illustrated by Betty Middleton-Sanford. Baltimore: Puffin Books, 1958 (see Green, *Tales of the Greeks and Trojans*).

143.   Green, Roger Lancelyn. *Tales of the Greek Heroes*. Illustrated by
        Betty Middleton-Sanford. Baltimore: Puffin Books, 1958 (see next
        entry).

144.   Green, Roger Lancelyn. *Tales of the Greeks and Trojans*. Illustrated
        by Janet and Anne Grahame Johnstone. London: Purnell and Sons,
        Ltd., 1963.

        All of the major myths associated with the Trojan War from the
        awarding of the apple of Discord to the homecomings of Agamemnon
        and Odysseus are found in this book. The text is divided into short
        chapters, each of which is copiously illustrated with deep-hued
        drawings of characters in moments of dramatic intensity. The first
        chapter describes the chief Greek deities (shown and identified in the
        accompanying illustration) and discusses the historical origin of the
        Trojan War stories. Green draws his material from later writers such
        as Dictys Cretensis as well as from Homer and the Greek dramatists.
        Unfortunately, half of the map of Odysseus' wanderings serves as the
        frontispiece of the book while the other half serves as the end piece.
        This book was first published in 1958 by Puffin Books (Baltimore) in
        two volumes entitled *Tales of the Greek Heroes* and *The Tale of Troy*.
        In 1963, the texts of the two volumes were combined and published
        under the title *Heroes of Greece and Troy* (New York: Henry Z.
        Walck, 1961). 5+

145.   Green, Roger Lancelyn. *Tales the Muses Told*. Illustrated by Don
        Bolognese. New York: Henry Z. Walck, Incorporated, 1965.

        The majority of myths in this book are etiological myths. There is,
        however, a section entitled "Greek Lovers and True Friends." In
        relating the stories, Green follows the basic plot line of the ancient
        source but tells the story in his own words, often increasing the
        proportion of dialogue. Careful attention is paid to detail in the black
        and beige illustrations. As on ancient vases, figures are identified by
        name. 6+

146.   Gringhuis, Dirk. *Giants, Dragons, and Gods: Constellations and Their Folklore*. Illustrated by Dirk Gringhuis. New York: Meredith Press, 1968.

Gringhuis presents myths developed by the ancient Greeks and Romans to explain a number of the major constellations. In his introductory chapter, he discusses the difference between astronomy and astrology; defines important astronomical terms, such as *equinox*; and theorizes about the origin of myths. Each of the subsequent chapters deals with a specific constellation, giving its story and location. Some non-classical myths are mentioned. Though he tells the stories in his own way, Gringhius does not contradict ancient sources. A key to pronunciation and a list of familiar constellations are placed at the end of the book. In addition to full-page black and white illustrations, there is a star map of each constellation, in which white stars are superimposed on a silhouette of the constellation.   4+

147.   Guerber, Helene Adeline. *The Story of Greece*. New York: American Book Company, 1896 (see next entry).

148.   Guerber, Helene Adeline. *The Story of the Greeks*. New York: American Book Company, 1896.

Guerber integrates into this elementary history of Greece brief retellings of the important myths and legends, which, as Guerber points out in the first chapter, provide "the only [literary] information we have about the early Greeks" (p. 12). These include foundation myths and the stories that constitute the Theban and Trojan sagas. When a Greek name appears for the first time, its accentuation and syllabification are indicated. Captioned line drawings aid understanding. This historical reader includes an index and two maps. The title of an earlier issue, copyrighted in the same year, was *The Story of Greece*.   6+

149.   Guerber, Helene Adeline. *The Story of the Romans*. New York: American Book Company, 1924 (originally published in 1896).

The myths which constitute an important part of Roman history, literature, and art are woven into this elementary history of Rome. They include the adventures of Aeneas and most of the famous legends in Livy's history. Writing "for very young readers" (p. 3), Guerber tells the stories in a simple and straightforward manner. Features of this historical reader include maps; a thorough index; and full-page, captioned, black and white illustrations. Though the preface announces that wherever a proper name occurs for the first time, the correct pronunciation is indicated, in reality, only the proper syllabification and accentuation are given.   4+

150.   Gunther, John. *The Golden Fleece*. Illustrated by Ernest Kurt Barth. New York: Random House, 1959.

Though much of what Gunther relates about Jason and the Argonauts is substantiated by ancient literary works, his retelling of some incidents differs radically from extant story lines; for example, after giving up his search for Hylas, Heracles swims from Mysia to the eastern end of the Black Sea and then walks to Colchis to rejoin the Argonauts. Gunther states that Jason fell madly in love with Medea the first time he saw her and that he was so happy with her that he did not mind the long trip home (p. 50). According to Gunther, after serving as king of Iolcus for many years, Jason finally fell out of love with Medea, whose use of black magic angered the Greeks. Each chapter of the book features several line drawings highlighted in shades of gray and brownish gold. On the inside cover is a map of the route of the Argo.   6+

151.   Haaren, John H. and Poland, Addison B. *Famous Men of Greece*. New York: University Publishing Company, 1904.

Recognizing the value of biographies, including mythical biographies, as a preparation for the study of history, the authors present, in language suitable for fifth and sixth graders, brief accounts of the lives of famous ancient Greek statesmen/heroes. The mythological figures discussed are Deucalion, Cadmus, Perseus, Heracles, Jason, Theseus, Agamemnon, Achilles, and Ulysses. Some inaccuracies result from the processes of simplification and bowdlerization of the ancient accounts. Most of the book's black and white illustrations are photographs of famous works of art. Each is captioned, and the artist is often indicated. The first time that a proper noun occurs in the text, its syllabification and accentuation are given.

The companion volume, *Famous Men of Rome*, features legendary figures whose stories are told in Livy's history as well as famous historical Roman statesmen, including Constantine the Great.   5+

152.   Haaren, John H. and Poland, Addison B. *Famous Men of Rome*. New
        York: University Publishing Company, 1904 (see preceding entry).

153.   Hall, Jennie. *Four Old Greeks: Achilles, Herakles, Dionysus, Alkestis*.
        Illustrated by Raymond Perry. New York: Rand McNally and
        Company, 1926.

        Hall relates incidents in the lives of Achilles, Herakles, Dionysus, and
        Alkestis. Attempting to make the characters as vivid as possible, she
        includes much fabricated conversation and descriptive detail. The first
        chapter is an introduction to Greek culture. All the pictures in the
        book were drawn from actual Greek statues or vase paintings. Some
        show scenes from literature; others, scenes from everyday life. Hall
        gives a pronunciation guide, a bibliography of primary and secondary
        sources, and suggestions for teachers, one of which is that students
        dramatize the stories.   4+

154.   Hamilton, Virginia. *In the Beginning: Creation Stories from Around
        the World*. Illustrated by Barry Moser. New York: Harcourt Brace
        Jovanovich, 1988.

        In her book of creation myths, Hamilton includes a paraphrase of
        Hesiod's account, including the castration of Uranus (Kronos "mowed
        down his father's love, and he dumped it into the sea," p. 130). In
        discussing Prometheus and Epimetheus, she combines information
        provided by several ancient writers. Her chapter on Pandora is much
        closer to Hawthorne (see Hawthorne, *A Wonder Book*) than to Hesiod.
        The illustrations in this book are striking and colorful but rather
        disquieting.   6+

155.   Hanlin, Jayne I. and Lichtenstein, Beverly E. *Learning Latin Through
        Mythology*. Illustrated by Hemesh Alles. Cambridge: Cambridge
        University Press, 1991.

        Each of the myths in this workbook are told twice--once in English
        (following Ovid who is nowhere mentioned) and once in simple Latin
        sentences with guiding illustrations. In addition to Latin vocabulary
        and exercises, the book includes suggestions for class activities, for
        example, directions for designing a board game based on the story of
        Atalanta and Hippomenes. An audio cassette of the stories in Latin is
        available.   6+

156. Hanson, Charles Henry. *Greek Stories Simply Told: The Siege of Troy and the Wanderings of Ulysses*. Illustrated with designs by John Flaxman et al. London: T. Nelson and Sons, 1884.

Hanson achieves the objectives he sets forth in his preface: "Of the cycle of epic poems in which they were embodied, only . . . the *Iliad* and the *Odyssey* have been preserved . . . But these epics present nothing more than episodes of a long story, though it is true that those episodes are the most important of the whole. The endeavour of the present writer has been to present the legends in one connected story, beginning with the founding of Troy, and ending with Ulysses' safe return and his vengeance on the enemies of his house. The story is told in simple language, and the Homeric narrative, so far as it covers the ground, has been faithfully followed" (p. v). Hanson generally accepts the most famous version of a myth. His first chapter includes comments on ancient Greek culture. A great number of line drawings are interposed throughout the text as are a few passages from Homer and Tennyson. The Latin names of the characters are used. The orginal edition of this book (1882) was entitled *Homer's Stories Simply Told*. The 1883 edition was called *Old Greek Stories Simply Told*. 7+

157. Hanson, Charles Henry. *Homer's Stories Simply Told*. Illustrated with designs by John Flaxman et al. London: T. Nelson and Sons, 1882 (see preceding entry).

158. Hanson, Charles Henry. *Old Greek Stories Simply Told*. Illustrated with designs by John Flaxman et al. London: T. Nelson and Sons, 1883 (see preceding entry).

159. Harding, Caroline H. and Harding, Samuel B. *Stories of Greek Gods, Heroes, and Men: A Primer of the Mythology and History of the Greeks*. Chicago: Scott, Foresman and Company, 1897.

Designed for readers at the third and fourth grade levels, this informative little book consists of short essays (3-4 pages each) on most of the major deities and mythical heroes as well as on many famous historical figures. The introduction to the historical section discusses the difference between myth and history. The authors provide a pronunciation guide, an index, and a few illustrations (none on mythological subjects). In their preface, they stress the value of the old

Greek stories "for the cultivation of the child's imagination and the development of the ethical perceptions" (p. iii).   3 +

160.   Harshaw, Ruth. *The Council of the Gods*. Illustrated by Nicolas Kaissaroff, Chicago: Thomas S. Rockwell Company, 1931.

In this novelette, Harshaw works descriptions of the Olympians into her story of Zeus' summoning of the council of the gods to discuss problems caused by Persephone's marriage to Pluto.   Harshaw elaborates on material found in the *Homeric Hymns to Demeter*, emphasizing scenic description and conversation rather than action. She indicates the pronunciation of a name when it first appears in the text and again in the index. Each chapter is introduced by a pertinent excerpt from either an ancient or a modern work of literature. These passages provide a challenge for the more sophisticated reader. Harshaw's introduction concerns the contributions of the ancient Greeks to modern culture. Quotations from the text serve as captions for the impressive black and white illustrations, which like the text, show great attention to detail.   5 +

161.   Hartley, Catherine Gasequoine (Mrs. C. G. Gallichan). *Stories from the Greek Legends*. Philadelphia: J. B. Lippincott Company, 1909.

Drawing from various ancient sources and sometimes combining material from them, Hartley presents a collection of famous ancient Greek myths. The first chapter is an introduction to the major deities and to the concept of deity. In retelling the stories, Hartley adds narrative details and invents conversations. At times her language is a bit archaic. Most of the illustrations in this book are black and white photographs of statues of mythological characters.   6 +

162.   Hawthorne, Nathaniel. *The Golden Touch*. Decorated and illuminated by Valenti Angelo. Mount Vernon, New York: Peter Pauper Press, 1939.

This is a limited edition of Hawthorne's version of the King Midas story (see Hawthorne, *A Wonder Book*). It was decorated and illustrated by Valenti Angelo and features large print. There are only 385 copies of the book. These were set by hand in Lutetia type and printed on mould-made Canson and Montgolfier paper at Walpole Printing Office, Mount Vernon, New York.   6 +

163.   Hawthorne, Nathaniel. *The Golden Touch*. Illustrated by Richard Salvucci. New York: St. Martin's Press, 1987.

This is an edition of the story of King Midas and the golden touch from Nathaniel Hawthorne's *A Wonder Book* (see below). Each page of text is alternated with a full-page, richly colored illustration. The illustrations resemble the illustrations in children's books of Bible stories more than the art works of ancient Greece. The distinctive feature of this book is that part of each illustration glows in the dark (making bedtime reading even more fun). 4+

164.   Hawthorne, Nathaniel. *The Golden Touch*. With foreword by Anne Thaxter Eaton. Illustrated by Paul Galdone. New York: Whittlesey House, 1959.

In the "Foreword," Anne Thaxter Eaton states that this version of Hawthorne's story is practically identical in wording to Hawthorne's retelling of the ancient myth of King Midas in *A Wonder Book* (see below). She notes that seven-year-olds like to listen to this tale while older children enjoy reading it for themselves. Paul Galdone colors approximately half of his drawings with orange and gold. The text is in large print. There is a special edition of this book for the Scott, Foresman and Company's "Invitations to Personal Reading Program." 5+

165.   Hawthorne, Nathaniel. *King Midas and the Golden Touch*. Retold by Freya Littledale. Illustrated by Daniel Horne. New York: Scholastic Inc., 1989.

This simplified retelling of Hawthorne's version of the story of King Midas from *A Wonder Book* (see below) is part of the Easy-to Read Folktale Series, which is designed for the beginning reader. As much space is devoted to illustrations (large and colorful) as to the text. 3+

166.   Hawthorne, Nathaniel. *King Midas: With Selected Sentences in American Sign Language.* Adapted by Robert Newby. Illustrated by Dawn Majewski and Sandra Cozzolino. Washington D.C.: Kendall Green Publications, 1990.

This adapted edition of Hawthorne's "The Golden Touch" from *A Wonder Book* (see below) is unique because it contains not only a written text and accompanying colored illustrations but also black and white illustrations that shows how the story may be presented in American Sign Language (which is introduced and explained in the introduction). A videotape that is coordinated with the book is available.   4+

167.   Hawthorne, Nathaniel. *Pandora's Box: The Paradise of Children.* Illustrated by Paul Goldone. New York: McGraw Hill Book Company, 1967.

This is a rendition of Hawthorne's version of the myth of Pandora, which is found in *A Wonder Book* (see below) under the title "The Paradise of Children." Paul Goldone's green and white illustrations invite careful scrutiny.   5+

168.   Hawthorne, Nathaniel. *A Wonder Book* and *Tanglewood Tales.* Volume VII of the Centenary Edition of the Works of Nathaniel Hawthorne. Columbus: Ohio State University Press, 1972.

Within the fictional framework of a college student telling stories to young acquaintances of Hawthorne, Hawthorne presents his version of various ancient Greek and Roman myths. In the preface to *A Wonder Book*, Hawthorne admits to "having sometimes shaped anew . . . as fancy dictated, the forms that have been hallowed by an antiquity of two or three thousand years" (p. 13). Not only does Hawthorne tamper with the story line, he also strives to substitute a Gothic or romantic tone for the classic one, which he finds cold. Moreover, he refuses "to write downward to meet the comprehension of children" (p. 4), who, he maintains, can understand lofty ideas as long as they are uncomplicated.

Hawthorne's version of the Pandora myth, which he entitles "The Paradise of Children," is very different from Hesiod's accounts (*Theogony* 570-612 and *Works and Days* 47-105). In Hesiod, Pandora is created as a punishment for man. Epimetheus accepts her as his wife. She has a closed jar (not a box) in which are all sorts of evils and hope. Out of curiosity, Pandora opens the jar. All the evils escape before the lid is closed again; hope, however, remains in the jar. According to Hawthorne, Epimetheus is a parentless child who is given an elaborately carved box by Quicksilver. Pandora, another parentless child, is sent to him to be his companion; but once she sees the box, she is consumed with curiosity about its contents. After going out to satisfy his passion for figs (not mentioned in any ancient source), Epimetheus returns to find Pandora about to open the box. Instead of stopping her, he says nothing, and so, says the narrator, is equally responsible for the troubles which flew out of the box. (Hesiod merely states that Pandora opened the jar; he does not mention the whereabouts of Epimetheus). The story ends with the release of Hope, who promises to console mankind forever.

Hawthorne's version of the myth of Midas and the golden touch differs from its ancient source, Ovid, *Metamorphoses* 11.85-193, in several ways. According to Ovid, Bacchus, god of wine, grants Midas the fulfillment of a wish for returning one of his followers, who in a drunken state has fallen asleep in Midas' rose garden. Midas requests and receives the golden touch but asks that the gift be taken back when he discovers his inability to eat and drink. To rid himself of the golden touch, Midas, following Bacchus' advice, bathes in the River Pactolus. According to Hawthorne, Midas is a greedy king who loves gold more than anything in the world except his daughter Marygold (a character created by Hawthorne). He is granted his wish for the golden touch by a stranger with supernatural powers. After accidentally turning his daughter into gold, Midas, now understanding that many things are more valuable than gold, wishes to rid himself of his golden touch. As in Ovid's account, he bathes in a river to lose his power but then uses water from the river to change all the things that he has turned to gold, including his daughter, back to their normal state.

This volume of the centenary edition of Hawthorne's complete works consists of both *A Wonder Book* (originally published in 1852) and *Tanglewood Tales* (originally published in 1853). It includes several editorial appendices. There are four full-page colored illustrations (captioned) and small line drawings at the beginning of each chapter. Many editions of *A Wonder Book* and *Tanglewood Tales* are available. The one discussed here was chosen because it is the most scholarly. 7+

169.   Hazeltine, Alice Isabel, ed. *Hero Tales from Many Lands*. Illustrated
         by Gordon Laite. New York: Abingdon Press, 1961.

         This anthology of heroic literature includes "A Cause of War" from
         Baldwin's *A Story of the Golden Age* (see above), "The Sack of Troy"
         from Church's *The Aeneid for Boys and Girls* (see above), "The
         Slaying of Hector from Church's *The Iliad for Boys and Girls* (see
         above), and "The Return of Odysseus" from Colum's *The Adventures
         of Odysseus* (see above). Hazeltine provides a short introduction to
         each selection, a glossary of unfamiliar terms, a pronunciation guide,
         and an index. The illustrations found in each chapter (some in color)
         are quite striking; the print is large.   6+

170.   Hewitt, Kathryn. *King Midas and the Golden Touch*. Illustrated by
         Kathryn Hewitt. San Diego: Harcourt Brace Jovanovich, 1987.

         This picture book contains a retelling of Hawthorne's (see Hawthorne,
         A Wonder Book) free retelling of Ovid's account of Midas and the
         golden touch. Hewitt uses simpler language and shorter sentences than
         Hawthorne. She changes some details and adds others, for example,
         a cat named Goldilocks. Many of the watercolor illustrations are set
         in frames.   4+

171.   Hodges, Margaret. *The Arrow and the Lamp: The Story of Psyche*.
         Illustrated by Donna Diamond. Boston: Little, Brown and Company,
         1989.

         In retelling the myth of Cupid and Psyche, Hodges abridges and
         paraphrases the account of Apuleius, whom she cites as her source. At
         the end of the book, she turns to the Neoplatonic tradition, relating that
         Psyche, when she became immortal, sprouted wings like those of a
         butterfly. At the beginning of the book is an annotated list of
         characters in the story as well as a paragraph explaining the connection
         between the butterfly, the soul, and Psyche. Many of the
         emotion-filled, deep-hued illustrations are reminiscent of the
         illustrations found in romance novels.   5+

172. Hodges, Margaret. *The Gorgon's Head: A Myth from the Isles of Greece*. Illustrated by Charles Mikolaycak. Boston: Little, Brown and Company, 1972.

In a smooth, rolling narrative, uncluttered by frivolous details, Hodges writes of Perseus' slaying of Medusa and his subsequent rescuing of Andromeda. Her description of the Gorgons is taken directly from Apollodorus. The book features large brown print on a tan background. The print goes well with the brown-toned illustrations, to which some may object because of the nudity in them. 4 +

173. Hodges, Margaret. *Persephone and the Springtime: A Greek Myth*. Illustrated by Arvis Stewart. Boston: Little, Brown and Company, 1973.

This book is a somewhat free retelling of the story of Persephone. Hodges portrays Persephone as the personification of spring: wherever Persephone treads, flowers spring up. In describing scenes and objects as well as in creating dialogue, Hodges employs her imagination. The large colorful illustrations which accompany the large-print text are rather fanciful, not to mention modernistic. Unlike the ancient versions of the story, this book has a light, optimistic undertone throughout, and its frontispiece features Shelley's famous line, "If Winter comes, can Spring be far behind?" 4 +

174. Hodgkins, Mary Davenport Hutchinson. *The Atlantic Treasury of Childhood Stories*. Illustrated by Beatrice Stevens. Boston: The Atlantic Monthly Press, 1924.

The only selection based on classical mythology in this anthology is "The Miraculous Pitcher" by Nathaniel Hawthorne (see Hawthorne, *A Wonder Book*). The editors do not indicate that Hawthorne is retelling a myth from Ovid. One captioned, black and white illustration accompanies the story. 6 +

175. Hollander, Paul (pseudonym of Robert Silverberg). *The Labors of Hercules*. Illustrated by Judith Ann Lawrence. New York: G. P. Putnam's Sons, 1965.

This is "A See and Read Beginning to Read Storybook" which features simple vocabulary, short sentences, and large print. Bowdlerizing a bit (for example, Hercules does not feed Diomedes to that king's man-eating horses), Hollander describes each of Hercules' twelve labors. In addition, he relates how the infant Hercules strangled two serpents. On each page, action-filled illustrations in pink, brown, and black on a beige ground visually present the material in the text of the page. At the end of the book, Hollander places a pronunciation guide and a list of key words, including *cowardly*, *hoof*, and *wrestle*.   3+

176.   Homer. *The Iliad*. Adapted by Diana Stewart. Illustrated by Charles Shaw. Milwaukee: Raintree Publishers, 1981.

In this condensed version of Homer's *Iliad*, Stewart manages to reproduce the tone of the original work as well as to include all of its highlights.   Very colorful, full-page illustrations are appropriately placed (several with a Greek alphabet border).   The last one, unfortunately, is inaccurate, for in it Hector's body is depicted as a skull. The book features easy language; large print; and a glossary of proper names, which is divided into three sections: Greeks, Trojans, and deities.   4+

177.   Homer. *The Iliad*. Adapted by John Norwood Fazo.   West Haven: Academic Industries, Inc., 1984.

This pocket book presents a condensed version of the *Iliad* in comic-book form--a form well suited to the action of the epic.   After a preface on Homer, the background of the Trojan War is related and then, without any indication of where the action of the epic begins, the major incidents of the *Iliad* are recounted.   The one notable omission is the parting scene of Hector and Andromache.   The point at which the epic ends is noted, but the book takes the reader to the end of the Trojan War.   Except for Zeus, who is always portrayed with two thunderbolts coming out of his body, the characters are appropriately represented in the illustrations.

The hardcover version of this book, a part of the New Age Illustrated School Series, has a "Words to Know" list (for example, *heralds*, *armor*, *curse*) and study questions at the end as well as footnotes throughout.   4+

178.   Homer. *The Iliad and the Odyssey: The Story of the Trojan War and the Adventures of Odysseus*. New York: Dorset Press, 1991.

The first half of this book is a condensed version of the *Iliad*; the second half, a condensed version of the *Odyssey*. Each chapter in the book is a greatly abridged and simplified retelling of the corresponding book of the epic on which it is based. The plot lines of the ancient epics are followed fairly closely though some details are changed, and dialogue is expanded. The character in the *Odyssey* whom Homer called Halitherses is called Alithene (p. 84). Aeolus is called Aeolius while his island is called Aeolus; however, the caption under the illustration correctly calls the island Aeolia (p. 108). At times, the tone and wording of the original work are reproduced. Introductory and concluding passages are added without indication of where the actual epics begin and end. Large, dramatic illustrations in water-color tones decorate every page. A sentence caption accompanies each illustration. The *Iliad* captions lack periods.   6 +

179.   Homer. *The Iliad: The Story of Achilles*. Translated by William Henry Denham Rouse. New York: New American Library, 1938.

In his preface, Rouse reveals that in preparing this translation of Homer's *Iliad*, he employed the same methodology that he had used in its companion volume, *The Odyssey: The Story of Odysseus* (see below). Though this book was intended for the general public, it is listed in the *Junior Books in Print* and is suitable for use at the upper-elementary level.   7 +

180.   Homer. *The Odyssey*. Adapted by John Norwood Fazo. West Haven: Academic Industries, Inc., 1984.

This finely drawn little comic book is a condensed version of the *Odyssey*. Though it ends with the reunion of Odysseus and Penelope and omits the Lotus Eaters, Ino, Argus, Scylla, and Charybdis, it includes most of the highlights of the epic. There is a preface about Homer.

The hard-cover version of this book, a part of the New Age Illustrated School Series, has a "Words to Know" list (for example, *swineherd*, *archery*, *minstrel*) and study questions at the end as well as footnotes throughout.   4 +

181.   Homer. *The Odyssey: Selected Adventures*. Adapted by Diana
        Stewart. Illustrated by Konrad Hack. Milwaukee: Raintree Publishers,
        1980.

        In this greatly condensed version of the *Odyssey*, Stewart focuses solely
        on Odysseus' actions. She includes most of the major incidents, but
        the Lotus Eaters, the Laestrygonians, and the visit to the underworld
        are omitted. Proper names are kept at a minimum. Stewart is careful
        to preserve the tone, the order, and some of the wording of Homer.
        She adds a glossary of proper names (with pronunciations indicated)
        and one of terms, for example, *loom, lyre*, and *whirlpool*. The colorful
        illustrations, partly because of their decorative borders, have the
        appearance of stained-glass windows.   4+

182.   Homer. *The Odyssey: The Story of Odysseus*. Trans. by William
        Henry Denham Rouse. New York: New American Library, 1937.

        Avoiding the lofty "poetic language" and affected tone found in many
        translations of Homer's epics but not in the epics themselves, Rouse,
        in translating the *Odyssey*, carefully chose English words that were as
        close as possible to the natural, simple words employed by Homer;
        however, he omitted stock epithets and reoccurring phrases where they
        were nonessential. Rouse added a summary-caption at the beginning
        of each book, footnotes containing commentary, and a pronunciation
        guide. In an epilogue entitled "Homer's Words," he set forth his
        philosophy of translation. Though this translation was intended for
        adults, it is listed in the *Junior Books in Print* and is suitable for use at
        the upper-elementary level. *The Iliad: The Story of Achilles* (see
        above) is the companion volume.   7+

183.   Hope-Simpson, Jacynth, ed. *A Cavalcade of Witches*. Illustrated by
        Krystyna Turska. New York: Henry Z. Walck, Inc., 1967.

        This book about witches includes two selections of especial interest to
        classicists: 1) the story of Jason and Medea in Colchis as told in
        Charles Kingsley's *The Heroes* (see below) and 2) a free translation of
        the second idyll of Theocritus by Hope-Simpson. Circe and Hecate are
        mentioned in the introduction, presumably under the assumption that
        the reader is familiar with them.   Black illustrations on a beige
        background enliven the text. This book was originally published as *The
        Hamish Hamilton Book of Witches*. London: Hamish Hamilton,
        1966.   7+

184.   Hope-Simpson, Jacynth. *The Curse of the Dragon's Gold: European Myths and Legends*. Illustrated by Alberto Longoni. Garden City, New York: Doubleday and Company, Inc., 1969.

Seven selections from classical literature, ranging from a condensed version of the *Odyssey* to a retelling of Ovid's version of the story of Proserpina to a selection ultimately derived from Lactantius' *De Ave Phoenice*, are included in this collection. As she states in her preface, except in the chapter on Theseus, where major alterations and additions are made, Hope-Simpson follows the story lines of her ancient sources (which are listed at the back of the book). She does, however, modernize the tone of the stories, which are illustrated with many modernistic line drawings.

This book was originally published in Great Britain as *The Hamish Hamilton Book of Myths and Legends*. Illustrated by Raymond Briggs. London: Hamish Hamilton, 1964.   4 +

185.   Hope-Simpson, Jacynth. *The Hamish Hamilton Book of Myths and Legends*. Illustrated by Raymond Briggs. London: Hamish Hamilton, 1964 (see preceding entry).

186.   Hope-Simpson, Jacynth. *The Hamish Hamilton Book of Witches*. Illustrated by Krystyna Turska. London: Hamish Hamilton, 1966 (see Hope-Simpson, Jacynth, ed., *A Cavalcade of Witches*).

187.   Horowitz, Caroline. See Strong, Joanna (pseudonym).

188.   Hutchinson, Winifred Margaret Lambart. *The Golden Porch: A Book of Greek Fairy Tales*. Illustrated by Dugald Stewart Walker. New York: Longmans, Green and Co., 1925 (originally published in 1907).

This book is unique in that Hutchinson's main source is the odes of Pindar. The title comes from the opening of *Olympian Ode* VI. Hutchinson combines information from several odes, adds material from other ancient works (She is careful to select only versions of myths current at the time Pindar lived), and invents many details. Besides treating of well-known characters, such as Jason and Castor, Hutchinson tells the stories of the Pansy Child (Iamus from *Ol.* VI) and the Fairy of the Rose Trees (Rhodos from *Ol.* VII). In her preface,

Hutchinson states that she follows Pindar's "maxim that 'disparagement of the gods is a hateful art'" (p. ix). The black and white illustrations in this book have an extremely florid quality. This edition is an expanded version of the book, which was first published in 1907.   6+

189.   Hutchinson, Winifred Margaret Lambart. *Orpheus With His Lute*. Illustrated by Dugald Stewart Walker. New York: Longmans, Green and Co., 1926 (originally published in 1909).

Inspired by Shakespeare's lines on Orpheus and his lute, (*Henry VIII*, Act 3, Sec. 1.3), which she used as a prologue to this biography, Hutchinson portrays young Orpheus as a child who eagerly desires to become a minstrel in order that he may move people through the power of music. Orpheus is instructed by the Muses, who tell him the stories of creation, of Prometheus, of Deucalion, of Apollo, of Demeter, of Cadmus, and of Dionysus. Having become famous for his songs, Orpheus meets Eurydice at the oracle of Apollo at Delphi, where he hears the story of Ion. Bitten by a snake on her wedding day, Eurydice dies in her husband's arms as he carries her over the threshold. In recounting Orpheus' descent into the underworld and his death at the hands of Maenads, Hutchinson stays closer to the ancient sources than she does in the rest of the book, where she elaborates greatly and changes parts of stories at will. The book ends with a comment on the immortality of music followed by lines 105-108 of Milton's *Il Penseroso*, which describe the power of Orpheus' music. The painstaking attention to detail in the full-page, captioned black and white illustrations causes the reader to linger over them. This edition is an expanded version of the book, which was orginally published in 1909.   6+

190.   Hutton, Warwick. *Theseus and the Minotaur*. Illustrated by Warwick Hutton. New York: Margaret K. McElderry Books, 1989.

In this picture book, Warwick Hutton makes equal use of text and illustrations (his own) to retell the stories of how Theseus retrieved a ring from the sea, how he slew the Minotaur, how he came to desert Ariadne, and how he inadvertently caused his father's death. Hutton adds much descriptive detail to material gleaned from various ancient sources (nowhere mentioned). He points out the connection between Aegeus and the Aegean Sea. Several of the richly colored illustrations show familiarity with Minoan works of art. One drawback of the book is that its pages are not numbered.   5+

191.   Hyde, Lilian Stoughton. *Favorite Greek Myths*. Boston: D. C. Heath
         and Company, 1904 (see next entry).

192.   Hyde, Lilian Stoughton. *The Great Stories of the Greeks*. Boston:
         Small, Maynard and Company, 1904.

         In her preface, Hyde states that she has selected those Greek myths
         "that have been world favorites through the centuries and that have in
         some measure exercised a formative influence on the literature and fine
         arts in many communities" (p. iii). The myths range from story of
         Prometheus to the labors of Hercules to Circe's dealings with Picus and
         Ulysses. Without mentioning ancient sources, Hyde retells the myths,
         adding descriptive details. She sometimes changes a plot line, usually
         in order to bowdlerize.   For example, instead of killing Argus,
         Mercury puts Argus to sleep. In the first chapter, Hyde discusses the
         religion of the Aryans and then introduces the Olympian deities. She
         uses the Greek names of the deities.   Hyde's book contains a
         "Pronouncing and Explanatory Index" as well as a thorough table of
         contents.   The subject and artist (whenever possible) are indicated
         under each of the black and white reproductions of works of art. This
         book was published by D. C. Heath and Company (also in 1904) under
         the title *Favorite Greek Myths*.   6 +

193.   Jacobs, Joseph, ed. *The Book of Wonder Voyages*. Illustrated by John
         D. Batten. New York: The Macmillan Company, 1896.

         The largest selection in this book of voyages to the "Land of Fancy"
         (p. vi) is "The Argonauts" from Kingsley's *The Heroes* (see below).
         Small but finely detailed brown on beige illustrations show scenes
         described in the story. The same shade of brown is used for the title
         of the selection and for the illumination of the first letter of the first
         word of each chapter in it. The other selections in the book concern
         the voyages of Maelduin (Celtic), of Hasan of Bessorah (Arabian) and
         of Thorkill and Eric (Norse). The preface and the scholarly notes at
         the end of the book are directed to parents and teachers.

         The latest reprint of this book is a Legacy Library Facsimile (New
         York: Legacy Press, Inc., 1967).   6 +

194.   Jamieson, Alan G. *Heroes, Myths and Legends.* Illustrated by Reginald Gray. London: Ward Lock Limited, 1978.

Three ancient Greek myths and one Roman legend are included in this book of selections based on heroic sagas. In "Odysseus and the Cyclops," Jamieson follows Homer closely, even preserving some of his wording. He does, however, have Polyphemus toast the first batch of Odysseus' men that he eats. Jamieson creates most of the descriptive details and dialogue in "Theseus and the Minotaur." He adds the story of the death of Talus, the standard version of which is told without mentioning the giant's name in "Jason and the Golden Fleece." The latter selection is highly condensed with some changes in detail. In "Horatius at the Bridge," Jamieson embellishes Livy's account. Each of the selections in the book has at least one colored and one black and white illustration of an action scene.   6+

195.   Johnson, Dorothy M. *Farewell to Troy.* Illustrated by Gil Miret. Boston: Houghton Mufflin Company, 1964.

In this juvenile "historical" novel, written in the first person, a grandson of Priam (created by the author) recounts his adventures during and after the fall of Troy. Most of the major characters associated with the Trojan War are introduced, and many insights into daily life of the Trojans are provided. The main character and his *paedagogus* find themselves in or hear about situations described in works of classical literature. The importance of the art of writing is a major theme in this book. In her epilogue, Johnson tells the reader about the ruins of Troy, mentions ancient accounts of the fall of Troy, and gives a brief history of the alphabet. At the beginning of each chapter is a small but detailed black and white illustration.   6+

196.   Judd, Mary Catherine. *Classic Myths: Greek, German, and Scandinavian.* Minneapolis: School Education Company, 1896.

Judd presents myths which enhance appreciation of nature. She often works a myth into an everyday situation. For example, in one story a child is reminded of the myth of Aeolus and Odysseus when her friends blow up a paper bag. The dialogue is a bit stilted, but the reader quickly becomes accustomed to it. Though she embellishes and bowdlerizes, Judd manages to stay fairly close to the ancient accounts. At the beginning of the book, she offers teachers suggestions for combining nature study and mythology. Each of the book's illustrations is of a single deity. 4 +

197. Kingsley, Charles. *The Heroes; or Greek Fairy Tales for My Children*. London: Macmillan and Company, 1879 (originally published in 1855).

This famous Victorian mythology book treats of three heroes--Perseus, Jason, and Theseus. Kingsley greatly expanded on information provided by ancient sources, inventing dialogue and description and injecting commentary. There are some inaccuracies; for example, Circe is Medea's sister rather than her aunt (p. 94), but no major restructuring of plot lines. Retelling the myths for his children, Kingsley, who was Rector of Eversley and Canon of Westminster, not only bowdlerized but occasionally allowed his religious sentiments to intrude into the stories. The strength of his religious conviction is apparent in his preface, which is addressed to his children and presents his views about ancient Greek civilization. The first edition of this work appeared in 1855. It had no illustrations and contained other works (for adults) by Kingsley, including a poem entitled "Andromeda." At the end of the preface of *The Heroes* section, Kingsley added an explanation of his method of spelling the Greek names. This explanation appears in some subsequent editions (of which there have been many) but not in others. In the 1879 edition delicate line drawings spotlight important scenes in the text.

The latest edition of this book (New York: Mayflower Books, Inc., 1980) is a photoreprint of the 1962 edition first published by Macmillan and Company in 1928. Illustrated by Henry M. Brock, it features full-page, captioned colored paintings as well as small black and white drawings. 6 +

198. Kingsley, Charles. *Theseus*. Illustrated by Frederico Castellon. New York: The Macmillan Company, 1964.

This is a reprint of "Theseus," the third story in Kingsley's *The Heroes* (see above). It features large print and many colored illustrations. In an afterword entitled "How Much Is True?" Mary Renault discusses the archaeological discoveries of Schliemann and Evans, which, of course, were unknown to Kingsley. 6 +

199.   Kinney, Muriel. *Stars and Their Stories*. Illustrated by Gabriel Pippet.
        New York: D. Appleton and Company, 1926.

        Each chapter in this book concerns the constellations visible during a
        particular month. Each contains a star map of the month, pertinent star
        myths, and instructions for locating constellations. The book begins
        with a note to children, urging them to begin with the current month
        (November is the first month treated) and to study the star groups one
        at a time. This is followed by a note to parents, suggesting that they
        point out constellations to their children and then read the appropriate
        chapter. In retelling the myths, Kinney greatly simplifies the stories,
        omitting as many proper names as possible and at times referring to the
        deities as human beings.   4+

200.   Kottmeyer, William, ed. *Greek and Roman Myths*. Adapted by Kay
        Ware and Lucille Sutherland. Illustrated by Edward Miller. St. Louis:
        Webster Publishing Company, 1952.

        This reader presents free retellings of some of the most important
        myths, including those of Perseus, Atlas, and Callisto. There are
        helpful explanatory comments, especially about etiologies. Information
        found in the ancient sources is expanded and (unfortunately) altered; for
        example, Ulysses puts wax into his own ears so that he will *not* hear
        the song of the Sirens (p. 135). In the chapters on Pandora and Midas,
        the influence of Nathaniel Hawthorne (see Hawthorne, *A Wonder Book*)
        is very evident. The first chapter provides an introduction to ancient
        Greek and Roman culture and to the Olympian deities. There is an
        annotated pronunciation guide at the end of the book. Many of the
        stories are preceded by a black on beige illustration which shows an
        important moment in the story.   3+

201.   Kottmeyer, William, ed. *The Trojan War*. Illustrated by Douglas
        Brown. St. Louis: Webster Publishing Company, 1952.

        This reader presents the story of the Trojan War from the Judgment of
        Paris to the reunion of Menelaus and Helen. Most of the book is a
        simplified and condensed version of Homer's *Iliad*. The number of
        proper names has been significantly reduced; the dialogue has been
        "modernized," and all domestic scenes have been omitted. The author
        adopts the spelling Phenix for Phoenix and Pirus for Pyrrhus. He calls
        the deities by their Roman names, which he thinks are more familiar
        and less difficult to pronounce. Except for his descriptions of the final

encounters of Patroclus and of Hector, where some details have been changed, Kottmeyer follows Homer quite conscientiously. He especially likes battle scenes. In discussing the events leading up to the Trojan War and those after the ransoming of Hector's body, Kottmeyer combines material found in various ancient sources (not mentioned), condensing greatly. He accepts the tradition that Apollo in his own person killed Achilles. Full-page line drawings help the reader visualize important scenes while the pronunciation guide helps in the mastering of names. Though the print is large and the vocabulary basic, there is a large amount of text in the book.   4+

202.   Kupfer, Grace H. *Legends of Greece and Rome*. London: George G. Harrap and Co. Ltd., 1909 (see next entry).

203.   Kupfer, Grace H. *Stories of Long Ago in a New Dress*. Boston: D. C. Heath and Co., 1897.

Intended as a supplementary reader for grade 5, this book features both prose and poetry. In her preface, Kupfer states that she wishes to familiarize her young reader with the mythological characters whom they "will meet again and again in art and literature" (p. 3). In each chapter, Kupfer, using the Latin names of the characters, retells a classical myth and then presents a poem on a related theme, for example, the story of Perseus in the floating chest and "Lullaby" by Alfred Lord Tennyson. With the exception of the hero tales, most of the stories are derived from Ovid, whom Kupfer follows faithfully though she does simplify and bowdlerize. Assuming the role of narrator allows Kupfer to comment on a character's motives and feelings as well as to inject explanatory remarks. The illustrations in the book are black and white photographs of well-known works of art (mostly ancient). A line from the text is placed under each illustration. There is a pronunciation guide. One error was noted (on p. 142), namely, that the Argo had a figurehead cut from an oak tree sacred to Juno (rather than Jupiter).

In 1909, an enlarged version of this book was published by George G. Harrap and Co., Ltd., under the title *Legends of Greece and Rome* and has been reprinted many times since then. The 1972 edition has only one illustration (the frontispiece): a modern-looking drawing of Jason and the dragon.

204.   Lamb, Charles. *The Adventures of Ulysses*. Edited by W. P. Trent.
        Illustrated with drawings based on the designs of John Flaxman.
        Boston: D. C. Heath and Co., Publishers, 1900 (The first edition of
        Lamb's work was published in 1807).

Intended primarily but not solely for children, Lamb's tale of Ulysses
is a paraphrased and abridged version of Chapman's famous translation
of the *Odyssey*. Lamb relates events in chronological order, adds many
explanatory comments, moralizes, and occasionally changes or inserts
details (for example, he states that Circe often visits the Sirens and
joins her voice to theirs). Because of archaisms and somewhat
sophisticated vocabulary, the young reader may need adult guidance to
properly appreciate this famous work. Trent's edition contains an
annotated pronunciation key, a map, 14 captioned drawings based on
the designs of John Flaxman, and a list of Lamb's chapters and the
books of the *Odyssey* to which they correspond. In a final note, Trent
presents insights into Lamb's life and literary philosophy. Trent's
edition of *The Adventures of Ulysses* has been reproduced as part of
Classics of Children's Literature 1621-1932: A Garland Series (New
York: Garland Publishing, Inc., 1977). It is included with the Garland
reproduction of *Visits to the Juvenile Library* by Eliza Fenwick, under
which title and author it is listed in OCLC.

There have been numerous editions of Lamb's work. The beautifully
bound 1912 edition (London: Thomas Nelson and Sons) has many small
line drawings placed next to the passages which they illustrate as well
as four full-page, painting-like colored illustrations with captions.   6 +

205.   Lang, Andrew. *The Adventures of Odysseus*. Illustrated by Joan
        Kiddell-Monroe. London: J. M. Dent and Sons, Ltd., 1962.

This book is a separate edition of pp. 1-171 of Lang's *Tales of Troy
and Greece* (see below). New illustrations, some in color, are added;
and the hero is called Odysseus rather than Ulysses. Roger Lancelyn
Green is the editor of this edition.

206.   Lang, Andrew, ed. *The Blue Fairy Book*. Illustrated by H. J. Ford
        and G. P. Jacomb Hood. New York: Dover Publications, 1965 (an
        exact reproduction of the first edition, which was published by
        Longmans, Green, and Company in 1889).

        In this book of fairy tales, Lang includes the myth of Perseus, retold
        as a fairy tale entitled "The Terrible Head." He uses no proper names
        for places or characters. Perseus is referred to as the boy; Andromeda,
        as the girl; Danaë, as the princess. The Gorgons are the Dreadful
        Women. In his preface, Lang cites Apollodorus, Simonides, and
        Pindar as his ancient sources. He includes a translation of Simonides
        543 without identifying it as such. Some dialogue is added, and a few
        minor narrative details are changed. Four finely drawn black and white
        illustrations show characters in the story. There are many editions of
        this work.   4 +

207.   Lang, Andrew, ed. *The Red Romance Book*. Illustrated by H. J. Ford.
        New York: Longmans, Green and Company, 1905.

        The myth of Cupid and Psyche, retold by the author's wife, is included
        in this collection of condensed romances. Leonora Lang's version of
        the story, which omits Psyche's last task (the securing of a box from
        Persephone), flows very smoothly and has a softer tone than Apuleius'
        account though his story line is followed rather closely. There are four
        colored illustrations with captions.   6 +

208.   Lang, Andrew. *The Story of the Golden Fleece*. Illustrated by Mills
        Thompson. Philadelphia: Henry Altemus Company, 1903.

        Beginning "Once upon a time there was a king," Lang, writing as a
        storyteller, presents in very smooth-flowing prose, first the myth of
        Phrixus and Helle and then a biography of Jason. Lang blends material
        from various ancient sources. These are not cited, but the influence of
        Apollonius' *Argonautica* is especially evident. Lang makes some
        changes in narrative detail, the most flagrant of which is his substitution
        of Nephele for Themisto as the woman whose children Ino
        unintentionally spared while unwittingly killing her own (cf. Hyginus,
        Fabulae 4). Lang calls the nymphs fairies and includes other
        anachronisms; for example, Medea fears that if her father learns that
        she has helped Jason, he will "burn her for a witch" (p. 71). A line
        quoted from the text explains each of the full-page black and white
        illustrations.   5 +

209.   Lang, Andrew. *Tales of Troy and Greece*. Illustrated by H. J. Ford. London: Faber and Faber, 1971, (originally published in 1907).

Combining mythological incidents gleaned from a wide range of ancient authors, ranging from Homer to Quintus Smyrnaeus, and filling in gaps and details with his imagination, Lang tells the story of the Trojan War and its aftermath, using Ulysses as his focal point. Then he relates the myths associated with the Golden Fleece (see preceding entry), with Theseus, and with Perseus (Bellerophontes' story is woven into that of Perseus). Lang arbitrarily alters narrative details. Writing as a narrator allows Lang to comment on the action, give alternative versions, and add elaborate descriptions derived in part from accounts of archaeological finds. A map shows important places mentioned in the text. The black and white illustrations have an almost cartoonlike quality. The chapter entitled "The Story of the Golden Fleece" had been published separately in 1903.   5+

210.   Lattimore, Deborah Nourse. *The Prince and the Golden Ax: A Minoan Tale*. New York: Harper and Row, 1988.

This is a new myth created by Lattimore. It tells of how Akros, a youth from Thera, brought about the destruction of his homeland by angering the goddess Dictynna. The extremely colorful illustrations contain elements derived from designs in Minoan wall paintings. Though this is basically a picture book, the vocabulary in the text is a bit difficult.   4+

211.   Lee, Frank Harold, ed. *Folk Tales of All Nations*. New York: Tudor Publishing Company, 1930.

Four excerpts from Lilian Stoughton Hyde's *Favorite Greek Myths* (see above) represent ancient Greek mythology in this anthology of folk tales from around the world. They are "Ceres and Proserpine," "The Return of Proserpine," "The King and the Oak" (Erysichthon), and "Psyche." The introduction to the whole book discusses the general characteristics of folk tales while the introduction to the section on Greek mythology points out that ancient Greek myths are characterized by freedom, art, joy, beauty, and heroes with supernatural powers. This book has no illustrations.   6+

212.   Leipold, L. Edmond. *Folk Tales of Greece.* Minneapolis: T. S. Denison and Company, Inc., 1970.

Leipold freely retells some of the most famous classical myths. He adds to the material found in the ancient sources; for example, he says that Daedalus sent a messenger to China to learn about gunpowder. He arbitrarily changes elements of stories; for example, he claims that Foreboding (rather than Hope) was in Pandora's box (not jar). Leipold makes one egregious error--in the chapter entitled "How Perseus Killed the Minotaur," he tells the story of Theseus but calls him Perseus throughout. A violet-colored illustration, bordered with a Greek key design, is placed at the beginning of each chapter. It shows an important character in the chapter.   4 +

213.   Lewis, Brenda Ralph. *Greek Myth and Legend.* East Sussex, England: Wayland Publishers Limited, 1979.

Much valuable information is provided by this little book, which is divided into five chapters: "Gods and Goddesses," "Heroes and Heroines," "Tales of Love," "Beasts and Monsters," and "History as Legend." Each chapter consists of a short introduction followed by paragraphs of description and interpretation relating to various pertinent characters and topics. This arrangement encourages browsing. Lewis draws indiscriminately from early and late, well-known and obscure sources. As a result, some statements, such as the following, are not substantiated by major classical authors: 1) Hope is a beautiful girl placed in a box by Prometheus, and 2) sea monsters (serpents are shown in the accompanying illustration) killed Laocoon. The extremely impressive black and white illustrations are reproductions of famous works of art or drawings based on them. A few of the artists are mentioned in the text. At the end of the book, the author has placed a list of derivatives and their meanings, a list of the major Greek and Roman deities, suggestions for further reading, and an index.   6 +

214.   Lewis, Shari. *One Minute Greek Myths.* Illustrated by C. S. Ewing. Garden City, New York: Doubleday and Company, Inc., 1987.

Shari Lewis, the well-known ventriloquist, presents parents with twenty condensed and simplified myths to read to their children in order to introduce them to classical mythology. Lewis begins with a note to parents. She includes a list of Greek and Roman names of deities (she uses the Latin names) and a pronunciation guide. Creation myths, hero myths, and many stories from Ovid are featured. No selection is over two pages in length. With few exceptions, Lewis follows the ancient sources. The colorful illustrations emphasize facial expressions.   4+

215.   Lines, Kathleen, ed. *The Faber Book of Greek Legends*. Illustrated by Faith Jaques. London: Faber and Faber, 1973.

This anthology presents a mythical history of the world from its inception through the Trojan War to the transformation of Lucius Apuleius into an ass. Some chapters are selections (edited to varying degrees) from children's mythology books, for example, Roger Lancelyn Green's *Tales the Muses Told* (see above), while others, for example, "The Tragic Story of Antigone," were written for this book. As a result, there is some variation in tone and proximity to the ancient sources. The foreword, written for adults, contains a brief survey of noteworthy editions of children's books on ancient Greek and Roman mythology. The last chapter is a discussion of some modern retellings of classical myths. Most of the book's black and white illustrations show scenes of action. There is an annotated index of names and subjects.   7+

216.   Lister, Robin. *The Odyssey*. Illustrated by Alan Baker. New York: Doubleday, 1987.

Lister makes this retelling of the *Odyssey* unique by making several radical changes in the story line. Despite the fact that Homer emphasizes Nausicaa's unwillingness to escort a stranger into town, Lister has Nausicaa lead Odysseus into the palace to the amazement of the Phaeacian nobles (pp. 10-11). According to Lister, Circe warns Odysseus that the Sirens will tear his flesh apart if he goes ashore on their island (p. 45). Lister also relates that the Sirens turned into "terrifying hags, half-woman and half-vulture" (p. 47) when they realized that Odysseus was not coming ashore. Lister imparts a modern tone to much of his dialogue, for example, the Cyclops asks Odysseus, "Who the hell are you?" (p. 24). When not exercising creativity, Lister follows Homer's *Odyssey* quite closely though he omits much of Telemachus' journey. The inside cover of the book is a map of Odysseus' travels. Eye-catching colored illustrations decorate most pages.   6+

217.   Little, Emily. *The Trojan Horse: How the Greeks Won the War*.
        Illustrated by Michael Eagle. New York: Random House, 1988.

        Designed for use in grades 2-4, this book features simple vocabulary,
        large print, a pronunciation guide, and many colored illustrations. It
        tells the story of the Wooden Horse and the fall of Troy. Sinon is
        mentioned but not Laocoon. The first chapter introduces the student to
        the physical make-up of Troy and discusses its strategic location. The
        last chapter concerns Homer and Heinrich Schliemann. This book is
        a Step 4 Book (grade 2 [advanced reader] to grade 4).   2+

218.   Low, Alice. *The Macmillan Book of Greek Gods and Heroes*.
        Illustrated by Arvis Stewart.   New York: Macmillan Publishing
        Company, 1985.

        Combining material from various ancient sources (not mentioned in the
        text) and generally following the best-known version of a particular
        myth, Low presents a compendium of Greek mythology. She includes
        creation myths, an introduction to the Olympian deities, stories from
        Ovid, a brief biography of Oedipus, hero myths, and constellation
        myths. In the "Foreword," Barry R. Katz discusses the nature of
        Greek mythology while in the "Afterword," he points out the difference
        between myth and legend and provides an introduction to Roman
        mythology. Features of this book include large print, numerous
        illustrations (many in color), and an annotated index. In retelling the
        myths, Low uses few complex sentences. She invents a considerable
        amount of dialogue and some narrative details.   4+

219.   Lowrey, Janette Sebring. *In the Morning of the World: Some of the
        Greek Myths Retold*. New York: Harper & Brothers Publishers, 1944.

        In her preface Lowrey states that one of her main themes is "the dream
        and its fulfillment" (p. xii). She centers her book on the idea (not
        found in ancient sources) that Zeus ordered Prometheus to create men
        suited to live during a Golden Age, but Prometheus dreamed of and
        then created men who by their "capacity for enduring toil and pain and
        sorrow would be able to substitute for the ease and pleasure of a
        vanished age, intelligence, courage, and nobility" (p. 22). These
        creatures finally win the approval of Zeus at the end of the book.
        Lowrey bases her retellings of myths on ancient sources but elaborates
        greatly and slants stories to fit her theme. She is the most literal in
        relating stories from the *Homeric Hymns*. Five chapters concern gifted

human beings while many involve beginnings. Full-page captioned line drawings show characters in action.   6 +

220.   Lum, Peter. *The Stars in Our Heaven: Myths and Fables.* Illustrated by Anne Marie Jauss. New York: Pantheon Books, Inc., 1948.

This informative book serves as an reference book as well as a general introduction to the stars. It is divided into three major parts--northern stars, zodiacal constellations, and southern stars. For each star group, Lum collects myths from around the world. In his discussions of Greek and Roman star myths, he often presents more than one interpretation, sometimes but not always citing his literary sources. Striking full-page black and white illustrations show star configurations.   7 +

221.   Lurie, Alison. *The Heavenly Zoo: Legends and Tales of the Stars.* Illustrated by Monika Beisner. New York: Farrar, Straus & Giroux, 1979.

The classical myths included in this collection of myths from around the world about animal constellations are the stories of the eagle (Aquila), the great bear, the lion, the water serpent (Hydra), the scorpion, the swan (Cygnus), the bull, and the sea-goat. The proper names Ursa Major, Leo, Taurus, Scorpio, and Capricorn are never mentioned. Aquila is described as the eagle sent by Zeus to strike Aesculapius with a thunderbolt. The sources (all secondary) which Lurie used are listed at the end of the book. A full-page, colored illustration accompanies each selection; and the table of contents features a diagram of each constellation. The book has large print.   4 +

222.   Mabie, Hamilton Wright, ed. *Heroes Every Child Should Know.* Illustrated by Blanche Ostertag. New York: Doubleday, Page and Company, 1906.

Mabie presents readings on heroes ranging from Daniel to Siegfried, from Robert E. Lee to Father Damien. Included are chapters on two ancient Greek heroes: "Perseus," adapted from Kingsley's *The Heroes* (see above) and "Hercules" by Kate Stephens. Stephens gives a biography of Hercules which emphasizes his first seven labours.

Mabie's introduction discusses the importance of heroes. There are no illustrations on classical subjects.

This book is also available in combination with *Fairy Tales Every Child Should Know* (nothing classical).   6+

223.   Mabie, Hamilton Wright, ed.   *Myths Every Child Should Know.* Illustrated by Mary Hamilton Frye. Garden City: Doubleday, Page and Company, 1914.

In this anthology of ancient Greek and Norse mythology, Mabie includes five selections from Hawthorne's *A Wonder Book* (see above); "The Cyclops," one of the easier selections in Alfred J. Church's *Stories from Homer*, a book for high school level and above; and "The Argonauts" from Kingsley's *The Heroes* (see above). In this edition, the full-page illustrations are colored while the smaller illustrations feature figures in silhouette.   7+

224.   Mabie, Hamilton Wright and Stephens, Kate, ed. *Heroines That Every Child Should Know.* Illustrated by Blanche Ostertag. Garden City: Doubleday, Page and Company, 1913 (originally published in 1907).

Readings about thirteen heroines, ranging from Paula to Pocahontas to Florence Nightingale, make up this book. The book's introduction concerns feminine heroism, pointing out that it is generally less dramatic but of a finer quality than the heroism of men. The only illustration in this book is of Joan of Arc. The selections concerning heroines in classical mythology--"Alcestis," "Antigone," and "Iphigenia"--are adaptations of Alfred J. Church's *Stories from the Greek Tragedians*, a book for high school level and above. In many places, Church simply translates the original Greek texts and elsewhere follows them closely. His language is somewhat archaic.   6+

225.   Mackenzie, Compton.   *Achilles.*   Illustrated by William Stobbs. London: Aldus Books, 1972.

Most of the myths about Achilles are woven into this biography of the hero; however, the famous story of how Odysseus proved that one of the "daughters" of Lycomedes was really Achilles in disguise is omitted. When two ancient versions of a myth are extant, Mackenzie sometimes combines the two into a new version. At other times, he chooses one version, not necessarily the best known one. For example, in describing Priam's visit to Achilles' tent to ransom Hector's body, Mackenzie follows a writer of late antiquity rather than Homer (No sources are specifically mentioned in the text). Mackenzie is in the habit of inventing superfluous information; for example, he identifies the plague in the Greek camp as dysentery. The name of Achilles' squire is spelled Patrocles rather than Patroklos or Patroclus. Mackenzie includes a genealogy of Achilles and a map of Achilles' travels. Large, somewhat modernistic illustrations in sharp colors break the monotony of the text. Each is captioned (often with a sentence lacking a period). This is part of a series entitled Golden Tales of Greece. In the United States, this book was published by World Publishing Company, 1972.   6 +

226.   Mackenzie, Compton. *Golden Tales of Greece: The Stories of Perseus, Jason, Achilles*, and *Theseus*. Illustrated by William Stobbs. London: Aldus Books, 1974.

This volume contains all of the mythological biographies which had been published separately as part of the Golden Tales of Greece series (see bibliographic entries 225 and 227-230).

227.   Mackenzie, Compton. *Jason*. Illustrated by William Stobbs. London: Aldus Books, 1972.

Mackenzie creates a biography of Jason by combining information given in various ancient sources (which he does not mention). In describing the relationship of Jason and Medea, Mackenzie basically follows Book 4.40-54 of Diodorus Siculus' *Library of History* but weaves in plot elements from Euripides and others. The resulting pastiche is not true to any one source. In Mackenzie's version, Jason falls in love with Glauke, daughter of the king Thebes (rather than of Corinth as in the ancient sources). Using the excuse that Medea had poisoned Corinthus, the king of Corinth, Jason divorces Medea. She sends his intended a bridal gown, which bursts into flame during the wedding. All the guests are consumed by the fire, but Jason escapes by leaping out of a window. Throughout the book, vividly colored painting-like illustrations are alternated with double pages of text. An explanatory caption (usually a sentence without a period) is placed in each illustration. The book includes a map of the route of the Argonauts and genealogical charts of the families of both Jason and Medea. It is part of the Golden Tales of Greece series. In the United

States, this book was published by World Publishing Company, 1972.   6+

228.   Mackenzie, Compton.   *Perseus.*   Illustrated by William Stobbs. London: Aldus Books, 1972.

Writing in the first person, Mackenzie catches his reader's attention by relating that he and some companions once rescued a Greek woman and her infant, who were floating in a chest at sea. He then launches into the story of Perseus. Skillfully piecing together information from several ancient sources (which he does not name), Mackenzie presents a complete biography of the hero. He creates narrative details and dialogue. The book ends with an explanation of the etymology of the English word *mycology.* A genealogical chart of Perseus' family and a map of Perseus' route are included. Large, strongly colored, painting-like illustrations arrest the viewer's eye, causing him or her to study the picture in detail. A caption (often a sentence without a period) verbalizes what is happening. This book is part of the Golden Tales of Greece series, which was published in celebration of Mackenzie's ninetieth birthday. In the United States, this book was published by World Publishing Company, 1972.   6+

229.   Mackenzie, Compton. *The Strongest Man On Earth.* Illustrated by T. Ritchie. London: Chatto and Windus, 1968.

This biography of Heracles includes all of the hero's major adventures and most of his minor ones. In addition, Mackenzie manages to weave in brief retellings of the myths of Echo, Narcissus, Persephone, Prometheus, and others. He gives a summary of the part of Apollonius' *Argonautica* in which Heracles appears (without mentioning the work) and a summary of Euripides' *Alcestis,* which he does mention. He carefully follows his ancient sources but does not hesitate to make editorial comments in the first person. In his prologue, Mackenzie introduces his young reader to the ancient concept of the world and to the major Greek and Roman deities. In his epilogue, he argues that Heracles was a human being whose exploits were magnified with the passage of time. Full-page line drawings show Heracles in action while the inside cover shows the Olympians.   6+

230.   Mackenzie, Compton. *Theseus*. Illustrated by William Stobbs. London: Aldus Books, 1972.

This biography of Theseus contains information not substantiated by any ancient sources. A major error occurs in the story of Hippolytus, Theseus' son. Mackenzie basically follows the account given in Euripides' *Hippolytus*. In that play, as in the other ancient sources, Hippolytus' complete devotion to Artemis angers Aphrodite, who punishes the youth by causing Phaedra, his stepmother, to fall in love with him. Mackenzie substitutes Athene for Artemis. Positive features of this book include large colorful illustrations with captions, a genealogical chart of Theseus' family, and a map of Theseus' route. The book is part of a series entitled *Golden Tales of Greece*. In the United States, it was published by World Publishing Company, 1972.   6 +

231.   Martin, Claire. *The Race of the Golden Apples*. Illustrated by Leo and Diane Dillon. New York: Dial Books for Young Readers, 1991.

Martin expands the story of Atalanta found in the ancient sources. She gives the bear who nursed Atalanta a name and relates that the bear had a cub named Odin, which Atalanta saved from a hunter. Martin connects the made-up hunting incident with the traditional race scenario by identifying the hunter with the Hippomenes, who later defeated Atalanta in a foot race. In describing the foot race, Martin basically follows Ovid's account, but she suggests that Atalanta allowed Hippomenes to win and ends the story with his victory. In Martin's version, Diana and her nymphs play an important part in Atalanta's childhood. Throughout her book, Martin capitalizes the word *goddess*. As the illustrators intended, the large richly colored pictures which decorate every page resemble medieval tapestries. Many of the costumes are medieval, but Atalanta's running outfit has a 1990s look to it.   4 +

232.   Marvin, F. S. *The Story of the Iliad*. London: J. M. Dent and Sons, Ltd., c. 1900.

This book is the companion volume to *The Adventures of Odysseus* by F. S. Marvin, R. J. G. Mayor, and F. M. Stawell (see the next entry). It is not currently available through interlibrary loan.

233. Marvin, F. S.; Mayor, R. J. G.; and Stawell, F. M. *The Adventures of Odysseus*. Illustrated by Chas Robinson. London: J. M. Dent and Co., 1900.

In their preface, the authors state that their objective was to reproduce in simple English, with some compression and omission, the substance and spirit of the *Odyssey*. The resulting work is faithful to the original. Each chapter is an abridged translation of the corresponding book of the *Odyssey*. The only major change is the substitution of the name Sea-kings for Phaeacians. Finely detailed line drawings with captions serve as illustrations. The frontispiece is in color.   6+

234. McDermott, Gerald. *Daughter of Earth: A Roman Myth*. Illustrated by Gerald McDermott. New York, Delecorte Press, 1984.

McDermott bases his version of the Proserpina myth on Ovid's account; however, he makes Ceres more of a matriarchal mother goddess than Ovid does. He also changes some details. All the pages of this book are tinted and have illustrations which focus on both action and emotion.   4+

235. McDermott, Gerald. *Sun Flight*. New York: Four Winds Press, 1980.

In this unusual picture book, vividly colored, ultra-modern illustrations visually tell the myth of Daedalus and Icarus. The superimposed text, kept to a minimum with all background information omitted, emphasizes the drama of the story. McDermott adds details not in any ancient works; for example, ghosts and monsters are imprisoned in the labyrinth with Daedalus and Icarus. The vocabulary in this book is quite sophisticated.   6+

236. McFee, Inez Nellie. *A Treasury of Flower Stories*. New York: T. Y. Crowell, 1921.

This book provides both scientific and mythological information about flowers of various kinds. The ancient Greek and Roman myths which are included are those of Adonis, Clytie, Hyacinthus, and Odysseus and the Lotus Eaters. They are accurately related. McFee alludes to the story of Narcissus and includes a post-classical myth about Iris.   6+

237.   McKissack, Patricia and McKissack, Fredrick. *King Midas and His Gold*. Illustrated by Tom Dunnington. Chicago: Children's Press, 1986.

Part of a series called "Start-off Stories," this book was specifically designed for the beginning reader. At the end of the text, there is a vocabulary list and a note indicating the correlation between the vocabulary and the Dolch, Hillerich, and Durr word lists. The authors use the word *ping* first to signify that Midas has gotten his wish for the golden touch, then to signify the transformation of objects into gold, and finally to signify the return of things to their original state. Only the nucleus of this version of the myth comes from Ovid. No one is credited with fulfilling Midas' wish for the golden touch though the passage which discusses the wish is accompanied by an illustration that shows Midas and a court jester (an anachronism). Midas not only changes his daughter into gold as in Hawthorne's *A Wonder Book* (see above) but also his queen, his cook, and his dog! There is a medieval flavor to the illustrations, in which purple and gold tones predominate.   2+

238.   McLean, Mollie and Wiseman, Anne. *Adventures of the Greek Heroes*. Illustrated by Witold T. Mars. Boston: Houghton Mifflin Company, 1961.

The main adventures of Hercules, Perseus, Theseus, Orpheus, Meleager, and Jason are recounted in this book. Writing in short, clear-cut sentences, McLean and Wiseman avoid difficult vocabulary and unessential names. Their attempts to unify and simplify result in some inaccuracies; for example, they make Perseus an Argonaut and attribute oracular statements to magicians. Many action-packed scenes described in the text are depicted in trichromatic illustrations. There is a pronouncing index.   4+

239.   McLeish, Kenneth. *In the Beginning: Creation Myths from Around the World*. Concept and illustrations by Helen Cherry. London: Longman, 1984.

The first chapter in this book defines the term "creation-story." Each of the following chapters presents the creation story of a specific culture, ranging from North American Indian to Australian to Near Eastern (Biblical). A full-page, colored illustration accompanies each selection. The chapter on ancient Greek creation myths--perhaps because it is the author's "creative" reshaping of the materials found in the secondary sources listed in the "Acknowledgements"--gives a confused and misleading picture. For example, the Hecatoncheires are described as "a blend of rock and trees: they had stony bodies, a hundred branching arms, twig fingers and bark-skin" (p. 36). The student interested in accuracy would do better to consult the reference books listed in the note entitled "Some Books to Read" (p. 48). 6+

240. McLeish, Kenneth. *Odysseus Returns*. London: Longman Group Limited, 1977.

In this condensed version of the *Odyssey*, McLeish spotlights Telemachus, providing psychological insights not in the original work. McLeish follows the order of events in the *Odyssey* and, at times, especially in the dialogue portions, reflects its tone and wording. At other times, however, he changes the story line for no apparent reason. Three examples will suffice: 1) Aigyptios rather than Halitherses explains the omen of the eagles; 2) Odysseus' remaining men are killed on the island of the sun rather than at sea; 3) at the end of the epic, Laertes' and Eupeithes' men kneel and honor Odysseus as king of Ithaca. McLeish adds descriptive details. Difficult words, for example, *suitor*, are explained in footnotes. Preceding the text of the story is an illustrated and annotated list of characters. There are two large black and white illustrations. One is a montage of Odysseus' adventures on the way home from Troy; the other is a fight scene. A cassette tape of readings from the book is available. This book was designed as a reader for slow learning adolescents. 6+

241. Metaxas, Eric. *King Midas and the Golden Touch*. Illustrated by Rodica Prato. Saxonville, Massachusetts: Picture Book Studio Ltd., 1992.

Influenced more by Hawthorne's treatment of the myth of King Midas (see Hawthorne, *A Wonder Book*) than by Ovid's treatment, Metaxas created his own version, one dominated by golden butterfly imagery. Metaxas increased the Hellenic elements of the story by giving Midas, (who Ovid says was king of Phrygia) a daughter named Zoe, by having a messenger from Helios visit him, by having him dine on olives and figs, and by having him recall how a conch shell, before it was turned into gold, had sounded "*thalassa, thalassa, thalassa.*" Lovely illustrations in pastel tones decorate every page. Because of its rather difficult vocabulary, this book is more appropriately read to or with the young child rather than by the child. An audio cassette with narration and music is available.   4+

242.   Mikolaycak, Charles. *Orpheus*. Illustrated by Charles Mikolaycak. New York: Harcourt Brace Jovanovich Publishers, 1992.

The author recasts the myth of Orpheus, enhancing the material found in the ancient sources.   The songs he creates for Orpheus are adaptations of Lionel Salter's translation of Alessandro Striggio's libretto for Claudio Monteverdi's opera, *L'Orfeo*.   At the end of Mikolaycak's retelling is a discussion (post-elementary level) of the ancient versions of the myth of Orpheus and of the influence of the myth on art and music.   This is followed by a bibliography (all secondary sources and most adult level) and a discography.   The physical make-up of this picture book is quite impressive.   Portions of the text as well as the dramatic richly colored illustrations (some with text overlaid) are set on a navy blue ground.   *Caveat emptor*: Since all of the figures in the illustrations are either in the nude or very scantily clothed, with pectoral anatomy especially noticeable, the maturity level and sensitivities of the intended readers need to be considered before adding this book to a school collection.   7?

243.   Miles, Patricia. *The Gods in Winter*. New York: E. P. Dutton, 1978.

To properly appreciate this unique little novel, the reader must be familiar with the myth of Demeter.   In it, the twelve-year-old narrator tells of strange events which occurred while Mrs. Korngold (a 1970s equivalent of Demeter) served as housekeeper to his family until her daughter Cora (Kore), who had been kidnapped by Mr. Underwood (Hades), was returned to her.   Elements in the story correspond closely to elements of the Demeter myth found in the *Homeric Hymn to Demeter* and in Ovid's *Metamorphoses*.   Except for that on the dust cover, there are no illustrations.   7+

244.   Miller, Katherine. *Apollo*. Illustrated by Vivian Berger.   Boston: Houghton Mifflin Company, 1970.

Through her selection of stories, Miller presents a well-rounded "biography" of Apollo from his birth to his servitude to Admetus.   She discusses his loss of his son Phaëthon, his punishment of Midas, his love of Daphne, and his rape (explicitly mentioned) of Creusa.   Though

Miller does not mention her ancient sources, her retellings are close enough to their originals to be recognized by the classicist as based on the work of a particular author. Miller adds a wealth of descriptive detail. Her simplification of myths sometimes results in inaccuracies: the monster Python is said to have possessed prophetic powers, and the Greek name Hecatoncheires is translated "Giants." At the end of the book, there is a guide to the pronunciation of proper names. Brown-tone woodcuts illustrate critical moments in the text. 6+

245. Moffitt, Frederick James. *Diary of a Warrior King: Adventures from the Odyssey.* Illustrated by Bill Shields. Morristown, New Jersey: Silver Burdett Company, 1967.

The first and larger part of this book is an imaginary diary to which Odysseus adds entries as he journeys home from Troy. Moffitt follows quite closely the passage in the *Odyssey* in which Odysseus at a banquet in Scheria, recounts his travels. The second part of Moffitt's book, entitled "The Eagle and the Geese," is an abridged and simplified version of Books 17-23 of the *Odyssey*, ending at the point at which Odysseus tells Telemachus to depart so that he may prove his identity to Penelope. Moffitt includes a brief introduction, in which he discusses the Trojan War and Homer; a map entitled "Odysseus' Navigation Chart"; and a glossary, featuring thorough identifications and a pronunciation guide. The book's colorful drawings, which show key scenes, are well coordinated with the text. 6+

246. Morris, William. *Stories from The Earthly Paradise.* Retold by Charles Seddon Evans. London: Edward Arnold, 1915.

The stories in this book are simplified prose versions of stories from William Morris' *The Earthly Paradise.* Three, "Atalanta's Race," "The Love of Alcestis," and "The Doom of King Acrisius," are retellings of classical myths. As Evans points out in his introduction, for Morris "it is not the story so much as the embroidering of the story that is the essential thing" (p. 4). Morris adds a voluminous amount of detail but does not change the traditional story line. The only illustration on a classical subject is a line drawing of Atalanta. 6+

247.   *Mythology*. Houghton Mifflin Literature Series (Grade 7). Boston:
        Houghton Mifflin Company, 1989.

        This paperback reader could serve as the basis of a seminar on classical
        mythology. The editors reproduce "Daedalus," "The Fortunate King"
        [Admetus], and "Atalanta's Loves" from *Greek Myths* by Olivia
        Coolidge (see above) and "Echo and Narcissus" from *Tales from Greek
        Mythology* by Katherine Pyle (see below). Each selection is followed
        by thought-provoking questions, for example, "Why did Daedalus
        achieve his goal and Icarus fail? What do you think this says about the
        Greeks' idea of proper human conduct?" At the end of the selection is
        a set of questions for a roundtable discussion of all the myths.
        Included in the book are a brief introduction to classical mythology, a
        note about Coolidge and Pyle, and an illustrated glossary of difficult
        terms, for example, *hovel*. Footnotes give proper pronunciation and
        other useful information. A full-page illustration, colored in rich tones,
        precedes each selection.   7 +

248.   Naden, Corinne J. *Jason and the Golden Fleece*. Illustrated by Robert
        Baxter. Mahwah, New Jersey: Troll Associates, 1981.

        This book is really a mini-biography of Jason that ends with Zeus'
        making the prow of the Argo, which had killed Jason, into a
        constellation. Jason's divorce from Medea and her attack on the
        Corinthian princess are mentioned, but Medea's killing of her sons is
        omitted. The author's attempt to simplify results in a few inaccuracies;
        but, on the whole, the book is true to the ancient sources and provides
        a good introduction to Jason. A large colorful illustration and a small
        amount of text (in large print) are found on each page. There is a
        pronunciation guide at the beginning of the book.   4 +

249.   Naden, Corinne J. *Pegasus the Winged Horse*. Illustrated by Robert
        Baxter. Mahwah, New Jersey: Troll Associates, 1981.

        Naden introduces the young reader to Pegasus and his rider,
        Bellerophon. In this version of the story of Bellerophon, Naden
        combines material from various ancient sources rather than following
        one account. Naden says that Bellerophon thought of himself as a god
        and that he was primarily motivated by a desire for fame--ideas perhaps
        implied but not specifically stated in ancient sources. In the colorful
        illustrations, which make the book visually attractive, the Chimaera is

depicted without the goat's head in the middle of its back, which it has in several ancient works of art.   4+

250.   Naden, Corinne J. *Perseus and Medusa*. Illustrated by Robert Baxter. Mahwah, New Jersey: Troll Associates, 1981.

Naden's biography of Perseus seems to be a simplified and abridged version of Apollodorus' account.   Naden provides psychological insights and invents dialogue.   She states that the Gorgons have the bodies of birds, but Apollodorus only says that they have golden wings and brazen hands.   Three-fourths of every page in this book consists of a colorful illustration which shows an action scene described in the accompanying large-print text.   There is a pronunciation guide at the beginning of the book.   4+

251.   Naden, Corinne J. *Theseus and the Minotaur*. Illustrated by Robert Baxter. Mahwah, New Jersey: Troll Associates, 1981.

This book recounts the life of Theseus, from his lifting of the stone to his assuming the throne of Athens.   Naden presents a balanced view of the hero, showing weak moments as well as triumphs.   Naden changes some details, but, for the most part, draws material from the ancient sources.   Features of this book include a pronunciation guide, which is placed at the beginning of the text; illustrations that look like water color paintings, and a large-print text, only a small amount of which appears on each page.   4+

252.   Newman, Robert. *The Twelve Labours of Hercules*. Illustrated by Charles Keeping. New York: Thomas Y. Crowell Company, 1972.

Combining material from various ancient sources (though no sources are mentioned in the book), Newman presents a fairly comprehensive and very lively biography of Hercules.   Newman treats the conception of Hercules in a straightforward nonsuggestive manner.   He places special emphasis on the twelve labours and omits the fact that Hercules killed his children in a fit of madness.   According to Newman, Hercules was only betrothed to Megara, who died while he was in the underworld.   Newman adds that Hercules became so distraught when he learned of Megara's death that he ruined a temple of Zeus.   Each chapter contains at least one line drawing.   There is a glossary at the

end of the book.   One illustration shows a bare-breasted
Amazon.   8 +

253.   Olcott, Frances Jenkins, ed. *Good Stories for Great Holidays*. Boston:
        Houghton Mifflin Company, 1914.

In retelling the myths, the editor keeps her promise of staying as close
as possible to the original works.   She includes graded reference lists
for further reading.   The myths included in this volume are: "Cupid
and Psyche"; "Clytie, the Heliotrope"; "Arachne"; "Hyacinthus";
"Echo and Narcissus"; "The Choice of Heracles"; "The Speaking
Statue"; "The Horn of Plenty"; "Baucis and Philemon"; and
"Daphne."   4 +

254.   Olcott, Frances Jenkins, ed. *The Wonder Garden*. Boston: Houghton
        Mifflin Company, 1919.

Many of the one hundred fifty nature myths in this book are from
ancient Greek and Roman sources.   These include Bion, Hesiod,
Homer, Pindar, Pliny, Theocritus, and Vergil as well as Ovid and
Apollodorus. The chapter entitled "The Adventures of Cupid Among
the Roses" is based on Anacreon, Moschus, and Lucian. As she states
in her foreword, Olcott worked with reputable translations of the
classics rather than adaptations of them "in order to preserve their
classical features, as well as to emphasize the poetic elements" (p.viii).
At the end of Olcott's book may be found: 1) suggestions for teachers,
including a model program for teaching nature myths; 2) an old English
calendar of flowers; 3) a list of additional readings; and 4) a subject
index for story-tellers.   The book contains only one illustration (of
Cupid) with a classical theme.   6 +

255.   Oldfield, Pamela. *Tales from Ancient Greece*. Illustrated by Nick
        Harris. New York: Doubleday, 1988.

Oldfield uses the main plot lines found in the ancient sources (which
she never mentions); however, she changes details, sometimes with a
view to bowdlerization. Like Hawthorne (see Hawthorne, *A Wonder
Book*), she gives Midas a daughter. Pygmalion is advised by an old
muse. All of the participants in the Calydonian Boar Hunt, except
Meleager, are portrayed as male chauvinists. At the end of the book
are thumbnail sketches of the major Greek deities mentioned in the

stories. Each is accompanied by a small line drawing. The rest of the illustrations in the book are large, dramatic, and in color. 6 +

256.   O'Neal, Zibby. *By Jove Stories*. Ann Arbor: Aristoplay, Ltd., 1983.

In this introduction to stories that the ancient Romans told, O'Neal gives very succinct versions of the major myths, including those of the heroes, The Theban cycle, and the Trojan cycle. Bowdlerization is extensive. The first time that a proper name appears, its pronunciation is indicated in parentheses after it.   At the end of the book are suggestions for further reading, an index, a pronunciation guide, and an annotated list of the Greek and Roman names of gods and heroes. Without revealing the sources used, O'Neal combines material found in various ancient works, Greek as well as Latin. The classicist will recognize summaries of the *Iliad*, *Aeneid*, etc. even though the works are not mentioned.

This book is part of a game with the same title, which was created by John Lacey. It is for 2-6 players, ages 10 and above.   7 +

257.   Osborne, Mary Pope. *Favorite Greek Myths*. Illustrated by Troy Howell. New York: Scholastic Inc., 1989.

This book is an excellent introduction to Ovid's *Metamorphoses*. Osborne retells eleven myths from that work, plus Apuleius' "Cupid and Psyche." Osborne simplifies Ovid's accounts, keeping proper names at a minimum and omitting risque details; nevertheless, she captures the essence of the Ovidian narratives. Osborne provides an introduction that discusses what a myth is, a chapter that introduces Ovid and Apuleius, a chapter that identifies important deities and mortals in classical mythology, and a chapter that focuses on modern words with Greek origins. She also includes a bibliography and index. At the beginning of each story is a full-page, earth-tone illustration of an emotional moment described in the text. The first letter of each chapter is illuminated. 6 +

258.   Osborne, Mary Pope. *Pandora's Box*. Illustrated by Lisa Amoroso. New York: Scholastic Inc., 1987.

In this elementary reader, part of the Hello Reader Series, Osborne presents an expanded and simplified version of Hesiod's account of

Pandora and her jar (here described as a golden box). Added are 1) dialogue between Pandora and Epimetheus, 2) a section on Pandora's attempts to hide the box so that she will not be tempted to open it, and 3) insights into Pandora's feeling before, during, and after the opening of the box. The illustrations, done mainly in gray and yellow, provide a visualization of the story. In her preface, Osborne tells her young readers what the ancient Greeks believed about their gods and then relates the story of Pandora's creation (without revealing that she was made as a punishment for mankind). In a note at the end of the book, Osborne briefly discusses each of the twelve Olympians plus Prometheus. 3+

259.   Osborne, Will and Osborne, Mary Pope. *The Deadly Power of Medusa*. Illustrated by Steve Sullivan. New York: Scholastic Books, 1988.

Written in the style of a novelette, this large-print paperback book begins with the Oracle of Delphi's prediction that Acrisius' grandson will kill him and ends with a description of Acrisius' death. In between is the story of Perseus. The story line follows that found in ancient accounts; however, the authors create a large amount of dialogue. They also add many descriptive passages, psychological and/or moral insights, and a minor character called Carpetus. The Oracle of Delphi is referred to as a woman. Each chapter contains one full-page illustration featuring various shades of gray. 6+

260.   Osborne, Will and Osborne, Mary Pope. *Jason and the Argonauts*. Illustrated by Steve Sullivan. New York: Scholastic, Inc., 1988.

This paperback novelette focuses on that part of Jason's life between his departure from Chiron's cave in order to claim the throne of Iolcus and his taking possession of the Golden Fleece in Colchis. The introductory chapter gives the background of the Golden Fleece and discusses the possible historicity of the Argonautic expedition. Though the Osbornes do not mention any of their sources, they seem generally to follow the *Argonautica* of Apollonius Rhodius, including the Argonauts' encounters with the Lemnian Women (bowdlerized), Phineus, and Aeëtes as well as the disappearance of Hylas. They add many descriptive details and much dialogue. They make the love of Jason and Medea mutual. Full-page illustrations in tones of gray are coordinated with the text. 6+

261.   Palmer, Robin. *Centaurs, Sirens and Other Classical Creatures: A Dictionary, Tales and Verse from Greek and Roman Mythology.* Illustrated by Don Bolognese. New York: Henry B. Walck, Inc., 1969.

The first third of this book consists of brief descriptions and line drawings of approximately seventy minor but significant mythical beings. Following are somewhat free retellings of myths about some of the creatures, including Talos, Glaucus, the Sirens, and the Teumessian Fox. Palmer cites his ancient sources at the end of each story. The book also contains a short introduction and modern poems about Orpheus, the griffin, and satyrs, respectively. A brightly colored illustration accompanies each story and poem.   6 +

262.   Peabody, Josephine Preston. *Old Greek Folk Stories.* Boston: Houghton Mifflin Company, 1897.

Peabody offers a wide selection of classical myths which she draws from Ovid, Homer, the Greek tragedians, and Apuleius. Though she tells the stories in her own words, Peabody is faithful to the original works and adds few descriptive details. Peabody's prefatory note on man's relationship to earth is interesting. Her thorough index contains both a pronunciation key and brief identifications. This book was designed to complement Hawthorne's *A Wonder Book* and *Tanglewood Tales* (see above). It is part of the Riverside Literature Series, which includes those works.   6 +

263.   Perkins, Al. *King Midas and the Golden Touch.* Illustrated by Harold Berson. New York: Beginner Books, 1969.

Perkins' retelling of the myth of King Midas is closer to Hawthorne's version (see Hawthorne's *A Wonder Book*) than to Ovid's version. In this version, Midas has a daughter named Leela, who is inadvertently turned into gold. Midas is granted his wish for the golden touch by a strange little man. This book, which is intended for very young readers, features large print, short sentences, and easy vocabulary. Vividly colored illustrations, which show the characters in seventeenth-century attire, take up a considerable portion of each page.   3 +

264.   Perry, Walter Copland. *The Boy's Iliad*. Illustrated by George Percy Jacomb-Hood. London: Macmillan and Company, Limited, 1902.

Perry offers what in essence is a simplified translation of the *Iliad*. He adds explanations of technical terms. He also provides a thorough introduction (chapters 1-5), which both describes the events leading up to the Trojan War and gives a personal history of Achilles. The epilogue (chapters 34-41) takes the reader from the burial of Hector to the death of Priam. Captions appear at the top of every other page and at the bottom of the black and white illustrations. There is an index, in which the pronunciation of Greek proper names is indicated. The archaic language, which occurs most often in the dialogue sections, may seem strange to young readers at first.   6+

265.   Perry, Walter Copland. *The Boy's Odyssey*. Illustrated by George Percy Jacomb-Hood. London: Macmillan and Co., Limited, 1901.

In his preface, Perry states that *The Boy's Odyssey* is intended as a "stepping-stone" to Butcher and Lang's translation of the *Odyssey*, which is quoted throughout the text (giving the dialogue portions a somewhat archaic tone). After ten pages of introductory material (cause of the Trojan War to the fall of Troy), Perry presents the adventures of Odysseus in chronological order. He writes in simple language, adding short explanations of names and actions to enhance understanding. A headline at the top of each page provides a summary of its contents, and the finely drawn black and white illustrations are captioned.   4+

266.   Picard, Barbara Leonie. *The Iliad of Homer*. Illustrated by Joan Kiddell-Monroe. New York: Henry Z. Walck, Inc., 1960.

In her retelling of the *Iliad*, Picard stays close enough to the Greek original to give the reader a feeling of the style of the work. Illustrations are carefully coordinated with the text. Background material is provided in the prologue and epilogue, and there is a glossary of people and places.   7+

267.   Picard, Barbara Leonie. *The Odyssey of Homer*. Illustrated by Joan
         Kiddell-Monroe. New York: Henry Z. Walck, Inc., 1952.

         Much of the dialogue in this book is a close rendering of the
         conversations in the *Odyssey*. The narration covers all of the major
         events in the epic. In Part I, Picard, carefully condensing, recounts in
         chronological order Odysseus' adventures on his way home from Troy.
         In Part II, she introduces Telemachus and reveals his actions during his
         father's absence. In Part III, she describes what happened after
         Odysseus returned to Ithaca. The preface serves as an introduction to
         the epic. The black and white illustrations (some highlighted in aqua)
         include a map of "the world according to Homer." In the Great
         Britain, this book was published by Oxford University Press
         (1952). 7+

268.   Pollack, Merrill. *Phaëthon*. Illustrated by William Hofmann.
         Philadelphia: J. B. Lippincott Company, 1966.

         Pollack makes Ovid's version of the Phaëthon story into a novelette.
         He provides insights into Clymene's life as a dryad and focuses on
         Phaëthon's relationship with a nasty youth named Kylos (whom Pollack
         created). Epaphus is not mentioned, but the role of Cygnus is
         expanded. Many descriptive details and much dialogue are added.
         Modernistic ink drawings are scattered throughout the text. 6+

269.   Power, Effie. *Bag O'Tales: A Source Book for Story-Tellers*.
         Illustrated by Corydon Bell. New York: E. P. Dutton, 1934.

         Power has a fairly long chapter entitled, "Greek Myths and Epics,"
         which includes translated selections from Ovid and Homer. For the
         benefit of the storyteller, Power comments on the literary style of the
         authors as well as on that of the translators or adapters. She also
         includes a bibliography of sources for further reading in the area of
         classical mythology. 6+

270.   Pratt-Chadwick, Mara Louise. *The Fairyland of Flowers: A Popular
         Illustrated Botany*. Boston: Educational Publishing Company, 1890.

         This botany textbook contains some myths about flowers. Only a few
         sections pertain to ancient Greek and Roman myths: 1) an abridged
         version of Nathaniel Hawthorne's "The Pomegranate Seeds" from

Tanglewood Tales (see above), 2) two versions of the myth of Narcissus (freely told), 3) a poem on the myth of Hyacinthus, and 4) a modern myth relating how the iris flower came to be named after the goddess of the rainbow. There are many line drawings of flowers and flower parts but none of mythological characters.   6 +

271.   Pratt, Mara Louise. *Myths of Old Greece.* Volume III. Boston: Educational Publishing Company, 1893.

The stories in this book are very well suited for being read aloud to children.   Adding descriptive details and much dialogue without vitiating the original story lines, Pratt presents condensed versions of the myths of Orpheus, Hercules, Theseus, Daedalus, Atalanta, Castor, Aristaeus, Arion, and Ulysses (first one third of the volume). Some of the illustrations are line drawings.   Others are black and white photographs of works of art. Each has a caption which explains the scene and names the artist (when known).

Because the vocabulary is a bit sophisticated and because the diction reflects the language of the time period in which the book was written, less capable students may find this book somewhat difficult to read. The "Vocabulary" at the end of the book consists of a list of annotated proper names with a pronunciation guide.   Volumes I and II are unavailable.   7 +

272.   Price, Margaret Evans. *A Child's Book of Myths.* Illustrated by Margaret Evans Price.   With introduction by Katherine Lee Bates. Chicago: Rand McNally and Company, 1924.

Price retells in simple language thirteen classical myths. Most are from Ovid; however, the myths of Bellerophon, Alcestis, and Psyche are also included.   She adds both descriptive and narrative details and bowdlerizes but makes only a few changes in plot lines.   In her introductory essay, addressed to the young reader, Katherine Lee Bates waxes eloquent on the origin and significance of myths. The captioned colored illustrations in this large-print book have an old-fashioned look to them. There is "A Pronouncing Vocabulary of Proper Names" at the end of the book.

In the 1935 edition of this book, which is entitled *Myths and Enchantment Tales,* the myths of Jason, Perseus, Circe, Romulus, Midas, and Orpheus are added; the introduction is abridged; and the pronunciation guide is omitted. Hawthorne's influence (see Hawthorne, *A Wonder Book*) is detectable in both editions of Price's book.   4+

273.   Price, Margaret Evans. *Myths and Enchantment Tales*. Illustrated by Margaret Evans Price. Chicago: Rand McNally and Company, 1935 (see preceding entry).

274.   Proctor, Percy M. *Star Myths and Stories from Andromeda to Virgo*. New York: Exposition Press, 1972.

A treasury of information about star groups and their stories, this book may serve as a reference book as well as be read from cover to cover. In his introduction, Proctor presents a brief history of astronomy and discusses Aratus' *Phenomena*, his main source. In the succeeding chapters he discusses forty-nine constellations. In each chapter, he includes not only the Greek or Roman myth, if any, that pertains to the constellation being discussed but also well-known myths from other cultures. Proctor quotes passages from Aratus, Homer, Ovid, and the *Bible*--sometimes identifying the source, sometimes not. The last chapter of the book concerns theories about the Star of Bethlehem. The constellations are discussed in alphabetical order, and there are cross references. Pyrrha is spelled Pyrra (p. 19) while Actaeon is spelled Achtaeon (p. 55). For most of the constellations, there is a diagram of the star pattern and a line drawing of what the constellation is thought to represent.   7+

275.   Proddow, Penelope. *Art Tells a Story: Greek and Roman Myths*. Garden City, New York: Doubleday and Company, Inc., 1979.

Proddow discusses twelve works of art on subjects from classical mythology. These range from a red-figure vase by Polygnotos, which shows Perseus, to a Maiolica dish showing Actaeon to Paul Gauguin's *Leda and the Swan*. Each chapter is devoted to one work of art. Proddow tells the version of the myth that the artist followed; then she comments on both the artist and the artistry of the piece. Generally, the entire artistic piece is shown in a colored illustration, but its details are shown in black and white illustrations. Proddow rarely mentions the ancient literary sources of the myths and does not indicate which details of the original myth the artist changed.   6+

276.   Proddow, Penelope. *Demeter and Persephone: Homeric Hymn Number Two*.   Illustrated by Barbara Cooney.   Garden City, New York: Doubleday and Company, Inc., 1972.

In this translation and adaptation of the *Homeric Hymn to Demeter*, Proddow reproduces the tone and wording of the original work. Her vocabulary in rather sophisticated.   The colorful, artfully arranged illustrations tell the stories almost as effectively as the text. Mirroring the style of the ancient Greek vase painters, the illustrator sometimes indicates the name of a character next to his/her representation. At the end of the book are found a note about the *Homeric Hymns* and an annotated list of characters and places mentioned in the text. This is a good book for an adult and a child to read together.   6+

277.   Proddow, Penelope. *Dionysus and the Pirates: Homeric Hymn Number Seven*.   Illustrated by Barbara Cooney.   Garden City, New York: Doubleday and Company, Inc., 1970.

This translation of the seventh *Homeric Hymn* flows very smoothly and is quite literal. Large illustrations, especially striking because of their deep hues, present a visual version of each scene in the poem. At the end of the book, Proddow comments briefly on the *Homeric Hymns* and gives an annotated list of characters and places. This book is well suited for an adult reading together with a small child.   5+

278.   Proddow, Penelope.   *Hermes, Lord of Robbers: Homeric Hymn Number Four*.   Illustrated by Barbara Cooney.   Garden City, New York: Doubleday and Company, Inc., 1971.

Having abridged the *Homeric Hymn to Hermes*, Proddow translates, indicating major omissions by the use of space.   Simplifying only slightly, she remains as close as possible to the original text. Her vocabulary is a bit sophisticated in places, but copious colorful illustrations aid understanding. The book includes a short note on the *Homeric Hymns* and a glossary.   5+

279.   Proddow, Penelope. *The Spirit of Spring: A Tale of the Greek God Dionysus*. Illustrated by Susan Jeffers. Englewood Cliffs, New Jersey: Bradbury Press, 1970.

While in her translations of the *Homeric Hymns*, including that of Dionysus (see above), Proddow stays very close to her ancient source in both wording and tone, in this book about Dionysus, she gives free rein to her imagination. This book has the tone of a twentieth-century juvenile novel. Proddow gives Silenus, who identifies himself as a water sprite (p. 35), the satyrs, and Pan a much greater role in the story of Dionysus than the ancient writers did. For example, in Proddow's account, the sileni help Dionysus attack the pirates who have kidnapped him. Proddow also enlarges Hera's role, emphasizing her spitefulness. Proddow fills her book with long descriptive passages. At the beginning of the book, she places an annotated list of characters, some invented by her. At the end she has a glossary of "technical" terms, for example, *himation*. Proddow never mentions any of her literary sources. The seven illustrations in the book are wash paintings reproduced in halftone.   6 +

280.   Pyle, Katharine. *Fairy Tales from Far and Near*. Illustrated by Katharine Pyle. Boston: Little, Brown, and Company, 1922.

In this collection of fairy tales from around the world, the story of Cupid and Psyche is offered as representative of ancient Greek tales. Though she abridges and bowdlerizes, Pyle follows quite closely the account of Apuleius, who is never mentioned. The illustration that accompanies the story shows Psyche and Charon at the River Styx. A line from the text serves as the caption.   6 +

281.   Pyle, Katharine. *Tales from Greek Mythology*. Illustrated by Katharine Pyle. Philadelphia: J. B. Lippincott Company, 1928.

This book includes all the major ancient Greek myths and hero tales except those about the Trojan War. Pyle tells the stories in such a way that they are both interesting and easy to understand. Citing only secondary sources, she sometimes mentions alternative versions of myths in the footnotes, which are mostly explanatory. Some seemingly unnecessary deviations from and additions to accounts found in ancient works will distress the purist; but, on the whole, the book provides a good introduction to classical mythology. There is effective use of shading in the finely drawn illustrations, and they are captioned.   6 +

282.   Pyle, Katharine. *Where the Wind Blows*. New York: E. P. Dutton
        and Company, 1902.

        Pyle presents ten myths from around the world. The stories are
        supposedly being told to his grandmother by the wind. The last
        chapter, "Perseus," is derived from classical mythology. Pyle names
        Perseus' sword Herpé. She departs from traditional sources when she
        states that Cassiopeia angered Atergatis, queen of the fishes.
        Otherwise, her smooth-flowing account follows well-known versions of
        incidents, though Pyle does add narrative details. One captioned,
        full-page line drawing shows Perseus rescuing Andromeda.

283.   *The Quiz Kids' Book: Stories and Poems*. Illustrated by Richard
        Dawson. New York: Viking Press, 1947.

        This is a collection of materials chosen by the Quiz Kids of the radio
        program of the same name. It includes "Orpheus" from *Orpheus:
        Myths of the World* by Padraic Colum (a high-school level anthology)
        and "How Perseus Slew the Gorgon" from *The Heroes; or Greek Fairy
        Tales for My Children* by Charles Kingsley (see above).   6 +

284.   Raphael, Elaine and Bolognese, Don. *Drawing History: Ancient
        Greece*. Illustrated by Elaine Raphael and Don Bolognese. New York:
        Franklin Watts, 1989.

        The unique feature of this attractive picture book is that it not only
        provides insights into ancient Greek history and mythology but also
        gives instructions for making drawings based on ancient Greek models.
        Mythological figures mentioned in the book include Zeus, Odysseus,
        Helen, Pan, Athena, Artemis, and Pegasus. There is a companion
        volume, *Drawing History: Ancient Rome*, which focuses primarily on
        Roman history.   5 +

285.   Raphael, Elaine and Bolognese, Don. *Drawing History: Ancient Rome*.
        Illustrated by Elaine Raphael and Don Bolognese. New York: Franklin
        Watts, 1990 (see preceding entry).

286.   Rawlinson, Eleanor. *Introduction to Literature for Children*. New
        York: W. W. Norton and Company, Inc., 1931.

        This book contains one section on Greek myths and one on hero tales
        (Jason, Achilles, Odysseus). Each section has an introduction directed
        at the teacher who has little or no knowledge of classical mythology.
        At the end of each section, there is a bibliography, a list of modern
        uses of the mythic material, suggestions for study, and a guide to
        pronunciation.   6+

287.   Reeves, James. *Giants and Warriors*. Illustrated by Sarah Nechamkin.
        London: Blackie and Son, Limited, 1977.

        Stories of true devotion (those of Alcyone, Psyche, Baucis, and
        Eurydice) and tales of traveling heroes (Theseus, Arion, and Odysseus)
        make up this book. Reeves follows the ancient accounts closely. He
        unobtrusively adds numerous descriptive details and explanatory
        commentary. Sometimes he weaves one myth into another. In his last
        four chapters, which are, in reality, a summary of the *Odyssey*, Reeves
        manipulates the ancient material more. In his introduction, Reeves
        defines "folk tale," then discusses how curiosity, a quality associated
        with the ancient Greeks, led to the invention of myths which were later
        told in writing by such authors as Homer, Hesiod, and (after the
        Roman conquest of Greece) Ovid. Reeves includes a pronunciation
        guide and a map of ancient Greece. Interspersed at appropriate points
        in the text are small but detailed black and white drawings of actions
        mentioned.   6+

288.   Reeves, James. *Gods and Voyagers: Legends of Ancient Greece*.
        Illustrated by Sarah Nechamkin. London: Blackie and Son, Limited,
        1971 (see Reeves, James. *Heroes and Monsters: Legends of Ancient
        Greece*).

289.   Reeves, James. *Heroes and Monsters: Legends of Ancient Greece*.
        Illustrated by Sarah Nechamkin. Glasgow: Blackie and Son, Limited,
        1969.

        The three heroes that this book focuses on are Jason, Heracles, and
        Perseus. The myths of Demeter, Daedalus, Midas, and Daphne are
        included as well as an account of the creation of the world. In retelling
        the myths, Reeves frequently follows the intricate plot lines of Ovid,

which involve many accessory myths. Reeves provides an excellent introduction to classical mythology and its literary sources. He places a pronunciation guide and a map of ancient Greece at the beginning of the book. Line drawings with black shading show scenes described in the adjoining text.

The first part of this book has been published separately under the title *Gods and Voyagers: Legends of Ancient Greece* (London: Blackie and Son, Limited, 1971). The second part has been published separately under the title *Islands and Palaces: Legends of Ancient Greece* (London: Blackie and Son, Limited, 1971). 7+

290.   Reeves, James. *Islands and Palaces: Legends of Ancient Greece.* Illustrated by Sarah Nechamkin. London: Blackie and Son, Limited, 1971 (see preceding entry).

291.   Reeves, James. *The Trojan Horse.* Illustrated by Krystyna Turska. New York: Franklin Watts, Inc., 1969.

In this book, a "fictional" Trojan named Ilias recalls how he and his sister, who were children at the time, survived the fall of Troy. Reeves follows Vergil's account of the Laocoon and Sinon incidents. The deep-toned colors of the large, action-filled illustrations make them particularly striking. 5+

292.   Reeves, James. *The Voyage of Odysseus.* Illustrated by Eric Fraser. London: Blackie and Son, Ltd., 1973.

In this paraphrase of Homer's *Odyssey*, Reeves abridges almost imperceptibly, remaining very close to the original work. He rearranges the order of the books of the epic in order to tell the story in chronological order. The Phaeacians are called the Sea Kings. A pronunciation guide and a map of Odysseus' route are placed at the beginning of the book. The prologue summarizes the events leading up to the Trojan War as well as the events of the war. Reeves uses rather sophisticated vocabulary. The black and white illustrations show situations described in the text. 8+

293.   Reid Banks, Lynne. *The Adventures of King Midas*. Illustrated by
        George Him. London: J. M. Dent and Sons, Limited, 1976.

        The Midas-touch myth as related by Ovid provides only the nucleus of
        this book. Writing in fairy-tale style, Banks makes both the time and
        place settings of the story indefinite. Midas retains his golden touch
        and has a rose garden, but a little person/magician is substituted for
        Bacchus. The author stresses Midas' attempts to rid himself of the
        golden touch, creating encounters with a personified river mouth, a
        witch, and a dragon. In this version, though not in ancient accounts,
        Midas has a daughter, whom he turns into gold and later restores to her
        human shape. The magician, who turns out to be a handsome prince
        with no royal blood, falls in love with her. The somewhat comical
        illustrations in this book, some of which are in color, have a Victorian
        look to them.   4 +

294.   Richards, George Mather. *The Fairy Dictionary*. New York: The
        Macmillan Company, 1932.

        Originally intended for children between the ages of six and eight, this
        little book contains one-paragraph descriptions of various creatures
        mentioned in fairy tales and myths. Most of the important woodland
        creatures and monsters of classical mythology are included as well as
        general terms, such as *sorceress*. Richards often ends a description
        with a personal comment. Good-sized line drawings accompany many
        entries, and a colored centerfold showcases several creatures. There
        is an index.   3 +

295.   Richardson, I. M. *The Adventures of Eros and Psyche*. Illustrated by
        Robert Baxter. Mahwah, New Jersey: Troll Associates, 1983.

        Richardson gives a condensed and bowdlerized version of Apuleius'
        account that often reflects the tone and wording of the original work.
        The illustrations, which resemble water color paintings and are found
        on every page of this large-print book, focus on the emotional states of
        the characters. This book is also available in paperback.   4 +

296.   Richardson, I. M. *The Adventures of Hercules*. Illustrated by Robert Baxter. Mahwah, New Jersey: Troll Associates, 1983.

Richardson tells the story of Hercules' life from his birth, which enkindled Hera's jealousy, to his completion of the twelve labors. With very little elaboration, Richardson concisely presents material found in ancient sources. The richly colored illustrations found on every page of the book help the young reader visualize the action. The text is in large print. This book is also available in paperback.   4+

297.   Richardson, I. M. *Demeter and Persephone, the Seasons of Time*. Illustrated by Robert Baxter. Mahwah, New Jersey: Troll Associates, 1983.

Drawing material from both the *Homeric Hymn to Demeter* and Ovid's *Metamorphoses*, Richardson presents the story of Persephone and then relates it to the change of seasons. Dark colors give the illustrations, which appear on every page of this book, a somber tone. This book is also available in paperback.   4+

298.   Richardson, I. M. *Odysseus and the Cyclops: Tales from the Odyssey*. Illustrated by Hal Frenck. Mahwah New Jersey: Troll Associates, 1984.

In this book Odysseus tells the king and queen who are his hosts about his adventures on the island of the Cicones, at the land of the Lotus Eaters, and on the island of the Cyclops. Richardson follows the *Odyssey* quite closely, reflecting its tone and style despite the fact that extensive condensation is required. Richardson keeps the number of proper names at a minimum; for example, the Cyclops is never called Polyphemus. On each page of the book, large, eye-catching illustrations in water-color tints show scenes described in the text. The cover illustration of the Cyclops will undoubtedly repulse some young readers while attracting others. This book is also available in paperback.   4+

299.   Richardson, I. M. *Odysseus and the Giants: Tales from the Odyssey*. Illustrated by Hal Frenck. Mahwah, New Jersey: Troll Associates, 1984.

This book is, in essence, a translation of a portion of the *Odyssey*. Odysseus tells the king and queen (no names mentioned) of his two visits with Aeolus and of his encounter with cannibalistic giants (Laestrygonians). Richardson retains both Homer's style and his tone. The text, in large print, occupies about one fourth of each page and is set either above or below exceptionally fine illustrations that resemble water color paintings. This book is also available in paperback.   3+

300.   Richardson, I. M. *Odysseus and the Great Challenge: Tales from the Odyssey*. Illustrated by Hal Frenck. Mahwah, New Jersey: Troll Associates, 1984.

In this book, Odysseus relates to the king and queen who are his hosts his problems with the Sirens, Scylla and Charybdis, and Helios. Richardson effectively manages to simplify Book 12 of the *Odyssey* and yet remain quite close to its text and tone. In showing scenes from the story in large colorful drawings, the illustrator pays special attention to the facial expressions of the characters. On each page, there is a limited amount of text in big, bold print. This book is also available in paperback.   4+

301.   Richardson, I. M. *Odysseus and the Magic of Circe: Tales from the Odyssey*. Illustrated by Hal Frenck. Mahwah, New Jersey: Troll Associates, 1984.

As its title indicates, this book, which may be described as a coffee-table book, focuses on Odysseus' two visits to Circe's island. Large, attractive illustrations that resemble water-color paintings invite study while the text preserves the tone and many of the descriptive details found in Homer's epic. This book is also available in paperback.   4+

302.   Richardson, I. M. *Prometheus and the Story of Fire*. Illustrated by Robert Baxter. Mahwah, New Jersey: Troll Associates, 1983.

Emphasizing Prometheus' benefactions to both mankind and Zeus, Richardson portrays Prometheus as a Titan whose spirit always remained free, even during the time he was bound to a rock. Prometheus' attempt to trick Zeus is not mentioned. As background to Prometheus' story, Richardson gives a simplified and bowdlerized account of the creation of the universe and of the change of power from Uranus to Cronus to Zeus. Richardson's portrait of Prometheus is a composite of materials drawn from several ancient and modern sources. The book features large print and dramatic illustrations (in color), which are closely tied to the text and appear on every page. This book is also available in paperback.   4+

303.   Richardson, I. M. *The Return of Odysseus*. Illustrated by Hal Frenck. Mahwah, New Jersey: Troll Associates, 1984.

The smooth-flowing text of this book focuses on the highlights of the last six books of the *Odyssey*.   Though simplifying a great deal, Richardson provides all essential information.   On every page, large illustrations that look like water-color paintings show the characters in action and suggest their emotional states.   Big, bold print is used throughout the book.   This book is also available in paperback.   4+

304.   Richardson, I. M. *The Voyage of Odysseus: Tales from the Odyssey*. Illustrated by Hal Frenck.   Mahwah, New Jersey: Troll Associates, 1984.

This book is a paraphrase in translation of the first eight books of the *Odyssey*.   Following Homer meticulously, Richardson includes all of the important incidents even though much condensation is necessary. The number of names is kept at a minimum.   Proteus is referred to as the Old Man of the Sea.   The physical make-up of the book is attractive.   Space is used judiciously.   The text in dark, bold print and the illustrations in water-color tones are well coordinated.   This book is also available in paperback.   4+

305.   Richardson, I. M. *The Wooden Horse: The Fall of Troy*. Illustrated by Hal Frenck. Mahwah, New Jersey: Troll Associates, 1984.

Centering on the story of the Trojan Horse, this book relates the highlights of the Trojan War saga from the dispute over the golden apple to the reunion of Menelaus and Helen as Troy was falling. Names are kept at a minimum. For example, Laocoon is called an old priest. Aeneas, however, is mentioned by name. Illustrations that look like water-color paintings take up more than half of each page. The print is large and bold; the sentences, short and crisp. This book is also available in paperback. 4+

306. Rivers, Robin, ed. *Questions Kids Ask About Myths and Legends.* Illustrated by Richard Comely et al. Danbury, Connecticut: Gralie Educational Corporation, 1989.

This book answers commonly asked questions about mythical and legendary matters. Questions on classical mythology include "Who had snakes for hair?" "What is a centaur?" "Who was Achilles?" and "What was the riddle of the Sphinx?" Each answer is several paragraphs in length; and nearly every explanation is accompanied by a vividly colored, action-filled illustration. Sometimes an extra bit of trivia, highlighted in blue and beginning, "Did you know that . . ." is added. 4+

307. Roach, Marilynne K. *Two Roman Mice.* Illustrated by Marilynne K. Roach. New York: Thomas Y. Crowell, 1975.

As Roach states in a note, this book "is a fairly literal translation of Horace's *Satire* II, vi, somewhat adapted for non-Romans" (no page). The illustrations, in shades of gray, were done by the author herself and show Roman objects mentioned in the text as well as Roman scenes. Roach includes the text which she is translating and a note (for adults) about Horace. The story of the city mouse and the country mouse, which Horace is retelling, is one of Aesop's fables. 4+

308. Robbins, Eliza. *Elements of Mythology, or Classical Fables of the Greeks and Romans: To Which Are Added Some Notices of Syrian, Hindu, and Scandinavian Superstitions, Together with Those of the American Nations: The Whole Comparing Polytheism with True Religion.* Pittsburgh: Hogan and Company, 1830.

While providing an introduction to classical mythology, this book also serves as an introduction to comparative religion (The author's comments reveal a Christian bias). The text is divided into small sections devoted to individual characters, both major and minor. The author interweaves remarks on the historical significance of various myths, on ancient Greek and Roman cultural institutions, and on relevant works of art. Heroes are called demi-gods. Captioned line drawings aid understanding.   8 +

309.   Robinson, Herbert Spencer and Wilson, Knox. *Myths and Legends of All Nations*. Garden City, New York: Garden City Books, 1960.

Each of twenty-two chapters of this book concerns the folklore of a particular nation, ranging from that of Babylonia to that of the United States. One chapter points out legendary figures and theories common to several mythologies. In each chapter, the authors begin with a brief introduction to a culture and then turn to its deities and finally to its heroes. The chapter on ancient Greek mythology, the largest section of the book, includes both the Orphic and Hesiodic versions of the creation myth. The section on Rome includes personifications, for example, Pax. The authors follow their sources so meticulously that they are recognizable to the classicist even if they are not mentioned in the text. This book may be read from cover to cover or used as a reference book. Although it is written for the general public, the book is easy enough for students at the elementary level to understand. There is a thorough index, in which the pronunciation of difficult names is indicated, but there are no illustrations.   8 +

310.   Rouse, William Henry Denham. *Gods, Heroes and Men of Ancient Greece*. New York: The New American Library of World Literature, Inc., 1957 (originally published in 1934).

Writing as a teacher telling stories to his class (which the preface reveals that he actually did), Rouse offers a brief but comprehensive survey of ancient Greek mythology, from the creation of the universe to the death of Pan. Drawing from sources as diverse as Homer and Nonnus, Rouse retells the myths succinctly. He does not change basic plot lines but does add explanatory commentary (there is a reference to man's evolution from monkeys on p. 13). As Rouse notes in his preface, he uses his imagination in creating dialogue. In his introduction, he distinguishes between the modern concept of God and the ancient concept of deities. Rouse provides a genealogical chart of deities and heroes. In this, the 1957 posthumous edition of his work, a "Pronouncing Index" has been added. The only illustration in the 1957 edition is the cover illustration of Icarus. The 1934 edition was illustrated by Norman Hall.   7 +

311. Russell, William F. *Classic Myths to Read Aloud*. New York: Crown Publishers, 1989.

With the objective of fostering "cultural literacy," Russell offers forty-two passages designed to be read aloud by parents. They are divided into two levels (ages 5 and up and ages 8 and up). At the beginning of each selection, Russell provides 1) a brief introduction to the mythical incident in the passage, 2) an estimated reading time, and 3) a vocabulary and pronunciation guide. He ends each selection with an etymological commentary. Russell bases his retellings only on secondary sources; but he chooses authors--Bulfinch, Mabie, and Church (cf. above)--who took pains to stay as close to the original works as possible. This book is also available in paperback. adult

312. Schneider, Nina. *Hercules, the Gentle Giant*. Illustrated by Tomie de Paola. New York: Hawthorn Books, Inc., 1969 (originally published in 1947).

Allowing her imagination free range, Schneider imagines what Hercules was like as a child--a gentle giant who liked to watch falling feathers. She relates how Hercules killed a fierce lion and frightened a cowardly king by appearing in a costume made from the lion's skin. Large illustrations in various shades of gray and blue visually tell the story. 3+

313. Schreiber, Morris *Stories of Gods and Heroes: Famous Myths and Legends of the World*. Illustrated by Art Seiden. New York: Grosset and Dunlop, 1960.

More than half of this book is devoted to ancient Greek and Roman mythology. Schreiber presents somewhat free retellings of most of the famous myths and hero tales (the sources of which are not mentioned) as well as greatly condensed versions of the *Odyssey* and the *Aeneid*. Though many details are changed, there are only a few major deviations from ancient accounts. For example, Narcissus, captivated by the beauty of Echo, rejects her because he thinks that she is mocking him; moreover, he thinks that he sees the image of a maiden in the pool (p. 33). Possibly as a result of a typographical error, the Pactolus River is called the Cactolus River (pp. 39-40). In the first chapter of the book, Schreiber discusses the origin of myth and introduces a few of the most important Greek, Roman, Egyptian, and

Norse deities. This large picture book features large, richly colored illustrations which encourage careful scrutiny.   6 +

314.   Schubert, Marie. *Minute Myths and Legends*. New York: Grosset and Dunlap, 1934.

Thirty-three sections on classical mythology are included in this collection of myths and legends from around the world. Each section is one page in length and contains a wealth of greatly condensed material about a god, a hero, or some other mythological character. In the "encyclopedia" at the end, the author provides a genealogy of the Greco-Roman deities and lists all of her many sources, only three of which--Hesiod, Homer, and Plato--are ancient Greek writers. Because of the author's great dependence on secondary sources, there are a few inconsistencies; for example, Rhea saves all of her sons, not just Zeus, from being swallowed by Cronus and, as in Hawthorne (see Hawthorne, *A Wonder Book*), Midas has a daughter. Each selection is illustrated with one or two carefully detailed drawings.   4 +

315.   Sedgwick, Paulita. *Mythological Creatures: A Pictorial Dictionary*. New York: Holt, Rinehart, and Winston, 1974.

Sedgwick gives thumbnail sketches of mythological creatures from around the world, ranging from Acephali to Maenads to Zombie. Creatures from classical mythology, including minor ones, such as the Lemures, appear on almost every page. The Muses are treated both collectively and individually as are the Fates. Various types of nymphs are discussed. Cross references are indicated by bold Roman type. On average, there are three line drawings per page. Though no sources are mentioned in the text, the author provides a bibliography, which consists mainly of secondary sources, though a translation of Ovid's *Metamorphoses* and one of Pliny's *Natural History* are listed.   6 +

316.   Sellew, Catharine Freeman. *Adventures with the Gods*. Illustrated by George and Doris Hauman. Boston: Little, Brown and Company, 1946.

This is a much simplified retelling of some of the most famous ancient Greek and Roman myths. When adapting Ovid, Sellew stays closest to her source. In the stories based on other authors, she sometimes changes important details; for example, in her account but in no ancient version, Vulcan is privy to Prometheus' stealing of fire. The preface of this book introduces the young reader to concept of myth; the index is annotated and includes a pronunciation guide. The vocabulary is basic. Colorful, full-page illustrations show scenes described in the text. 4+

317. Serraillier, Ian. *The Clashing Rocks: The Story of Jason.* Illustrated by William Stobbs. New York: Henry Z. Walck, Incorporated, 1964.

The primary emphasis of this "biography" of Jason is on the Argonautic expedition. Working from translations of the *Argonautica* of Apollonius Rhodius, the *Library* of Apollodorus, and the *Metamorphoses* of Ovid as well as secondary sources which are mentioned at the beginning of his work, Serraillier presents a smooth-flowing account. He condenses material and adds descriptive details without vitiating either the original story lines or the tone of his version. Although many place names are mentioned, there unfortunately is no map. On page 31, Peleus is written for Pelias. Each of the twenty chapters has a black and white illustration that reinforces an important passage in the text. 6+

318. Serraillier, Ian. *A Fall from the Sky: The Story of Daedalus.* Illustrated by William Stobbs. New York: Henry Z. Walck, Incorporated, 1966.

Serraillier blends mythological themes, drawn mainly from Ovid, and archaeological information into this action-oriented account of the life of Daedalus from his murder of his nephew Talos (Perdix) to the death of Icarus. There is much invented detail, especially in the escape scenes. Half-page lithographs show scenes from the text. 6+

319. Serraillier, Ian. *The Gorgon's Head: The Story of Perseus.* Illustrated by William Stobbs. New York: Henry Z. Walck, Incorporated, 1962.

Serraillier combines material from several ancient sources, primarily Apollodorus and Ovid, into a coherent biography of Perseus. He adds conversations, narrative detail, and descriptive passages of his own invention. The line drawings of scenes in the text are highlighted in black for maximum effectiveness. 4+

320.   Serraillier, Ian. *Heracles the Strong*. Illustrations by Rocco Negri. New York: Henry Z. Walck, Incorporated, 1970.

This life of Heracles flows along so smoothly that the reader barely notices that it is a composite of many disparate stories about the hero. The two Theseus incidents and the two Deianira incidents help to unify the plot. Heracles' encounters with Cacus, Antaeus, Prometheus, and Meleager's shade are included as well as the major events of the hero's life. The chapters on Heracles' madness, on the rescue of Alcestis, and on Heracles' final days closely follow Euripides' plays on those subjects. Serraillier omits the circumstances surrounding Heracles' conception; he does mention the hero's marital infidelity. Serraillier lists his sources at the beginning of the book. Each chapter has a black and white woodcut that illustrates a key scene in the chapter.   7+

321.   Serraillier, Ian. *The Way of Danger: The Story of Theseus*. Illustrated by William Stobbs. New York: Henry Z. Walck, Incorporated, 1963.

Deriving material from translations of Plutarch's *Theseus* and Ovid's *Metamorphoses* and other secondary sources which he lists at the beginning of his book, Serraillier weaves together a fairly comprehensive yet smooth-flowing biography of Theseus. As might be expected in a children's book, neither Hippolytus nor Phaedra is mentioned. Serraillier adds a large amount of dialogue and narrative detail; for example, he states that in the Labyrinth, Theseus lighted his way with a jewelled crown that Thetis had given him. Black and white illustrations show action scenes described in the adjoining text.   5+

322.   Sewell, Helen. *A Book of Myths: Selections from Bulfinch's Age of Fable*. Illustrated by Helen Sewell. New York: The Macmillan Company, 1942 (see Bulfinch, Thomas).

323.   Shahan, Thomas J., ed. *A Book of Famous Myths and Legends*. Young Folk's Library Series. Boston: Hall and Locke Company, 1901 (see the next entry).

324.   Shahan, Thomas J., ed. *Famous Myths and Legends*. New York: Derrydale Books, 1991.

More than half of the stories in this collection concern characters in classical mythology. There are selections from Nathaniel Hawthorne's *A Wonder Book* (see above) from Charles Kingsley's *The Heroes* (see above) and from Church's *The Odyssey of Homer* (see above). In the first chapter, Shahan distinguishes between myth and legend and comments on the significance of both. The first letter of each chapter is illuminated in black and white; and at the end of each section, there is a small black and white illustration. The book includes selections from English, American, and Irish literature. This book was originally published as *A Book of Famous Myths and Legends*, Boston: Hall and Locke Company, 1901, as part of the Young Folk's Library Series.   7+

325.   Shaw, Charles Dannelly. *Stories of the Ancient Greeks*. Boston: Ginn and Company, 1903.

This book is divided into two sections--mythological stories (ancient sources are not indicated) and historical stories, which the introduction states are drawn from Herodotus, Thucydides, Xenophon, and Plutarch. The author includes most of the major myths. He follows the ancient plot outlines but adds dialogue and descriptive detail. Features of the book include an introduction, which treats early Greek history; a table of contents; a thorough "index with pronunciations"; a map of Greece; and captioned line drawings designed to show action.   6+

326.   Shippen, Katherine B. *A Bridle for Pegasus*. Illustrated by C. B. Falls. New York: The Viking Press, 1966.

This book on the history of flight includes as its first chapter one myth--that of Daedalus and Icarus. Writing in the first person, Shippen retells the story, adding conversation and narrative details to material from ancient sources. She changes Daedalus' homeland from Athens to Sicily. Opposite the title page of the book is a passage about Pegasus from Hawthorne's *A Wonder Book*. Shippen obviously assumes that the reader is familiar with the myth of the winged horse.   7+

327.   Silverberg, Robert. See Hollander, Paul (pseudonym).

328.   Siekkinen, Raija. *The Curious Faun*. Translated from the Finnish by
        Tim Steffa. Illustrated by Hannu Taina. Minneapolis: Carolrhoda
        Books, Inc., 1986.

        A woodland creature from Roman mythology, the faun, provided the
        inspiration for this story, which relates the adventures of a young faun
        who (in modern times) leaves the forest to learn about human beings.
        In the large watercolor illustrations of this picture book, the fauns are
        distinguished by their big pointed ears, their main identifying
        characteristic in ancient works of art, too.   4+

329.   Silverthorne, Elizabeth. *I, Heracles*.   Illustrated by Billie Jean
        Osborne. Nashville: Abingdon, 1978.

        In this "autobiography," Heracles claims to tell the real story of his
        labors and to reveal his feelings "about all the awful and wonderful
        things that have happened" (p. 11).   In the preface, he discusses his
        childhood. Then he explains that his labors were carried out to atone
        for the murder of his wife and children. Worked into the account of
        Heracles' labors at the appropriate point are the stories of Alcestis,
        Hesione, Cacus, Busiris, and Antaeus. Features of the book include a
        map of the world of Heracles; a glossary; and action-filled, full-page
        line drawings.   Silverthorne does not mention her sources but her
        account follows Apollodorus' quite closely--with descriptive details and
        conversation added.   4+

330.   Simons, Jamie and Simons, Scott. *Why Dolphins Call: A Story of
        Dionysus*. Illustrated by Anthony Acardo. Englewood Cliffs, New
        Jersey: Silver Press, 1991.

        Incorporating many details found in the *Homeric Hymn to Dionysus*,
        the authors reveal that the god Dionysus turned pirates who had
        captured him into dolphins. To answer the question posed in their title,
        they state that Dionysus enjoined the newly created dolphins to guide
        seafarers in difficulty. The mention of tomatoes is an anachronism.
        The text of this picture book is superimposed over deeply colored
        full-page illustrations that focus on the emotions as well as the actions
        of the characters.   3+

331. Simons, Jamie and Simons, Scott. *Why Spiders Spin: A Story of Arachne*. Illustrated by Deborah Winograd. Englewood Cliffs, New Jersey: Silver Press, 1991.

Sometimes closely mirroring Ovid's account (which is not mentioned), at other times waxing eloquent with descriptive details, the authors retell the story of Arachne. They end their book with an explanation of the English word *arachnid*. The text of this picture book is superimposed over vividly colored illustrations.   4 +

332. Sissons, Nicola Ann. *Myths and Legends of the Greeks*. Illustrated by Rafaello Busoni. New York: Hart Publishing Company, 1960.

Even though this is a book of ancient stories, it has a modern tone and look. Sissons retells, in abridged and simplified form, many of the most famous ancient Greek myths and legends. There is a copious supply of eye-catching black and white illustrations, many of which have quotations from the text beneath them.   5 +

333. Skinner, Ada M. and Skinner, Eleanor L. *The Emerald Story Book: Stories and Legends of Spring, Nature and Easter*. New York: Duffield and Company, 1915.

The only classical myth included in this collection is that of Proserpina and Pluto. Remaining faithful to the ancient sources, which are not mentioned, Skinner retells the story in a gentle, easy-to-understand manner.   4 +

334. Skinner, Charles Montgomery. *Myths and Legends of Flowers, Trees, Fruits, and Plants in All Ages and in All Climes*. Philadelphia: J. B. Lippincott Company, 1911.

Although not a children's book, this tome would be a useful reference book in the elementary classroom. Skinner offers a great deal of interesting information about plants. He discusses 176 plants individually, including a description of each plant as well as historical and mythological tidbits. The plants are listed in alphabetical order. There are numerous references to ancient Greek and Roman mythology and culture throughout the book. Skinner recounts myths succinctly, often not mentioning his literary sources. In the first chapter, Skinner comments on the symbolism of plants and their influence on family names. The next three chapters treat early Christian plant legends, myths about narcotic plants, and stories of poisonous plants, respectively. Most of the illustrations are black and white photographs of famous works of art featuring plants mentioned in the book.   8 +

335.   Southworth, Gertrude Van Duyn and Southworth, John. *The Story of Long Ago*. New York: Iroquois Publishing Company, Inc., 1934.

This history textbook, designed for use in the elementary school, provides an introduction to ancient Greek and Norse mythology as well as an overview of western civilization from the Stone Age to the fall of Rome. Each chapter has an introductory note, a glossary, black and white illustrations with accompanying explanations, and study questions. The section on Greek mythology covers most of the major deities and heroes plus highlights of the Trojan War saga. As is to be expected in a book of this scope, all the myths are greatly simplified; but still a wealth of valuable information is included.   6 +

336.   Spickelmire, Corinne.   *Stories of Hellas*.   Indianapolis: The Bobbs-Merrill Company, 1911.

In this introduction to ancient Greek culture, Spickelmire includes both myths and historical information. In the section on bards and their songs, she gives the mythological history of Hellas from creation through the Trojan War. The Theban stories, however, are omitted. In her chapter on Greek religion, she describes each of the Olympian deities. She states that the Greek myths were composed by wandering bards.   Her comments on early Greek history and the Homeric Question reflect the scholarship of the time at which she was writing. Her book has a definite Christian bias.   Homer is the only ancient literary source that Spickelmire mentions though she derives information from many others. Several of the book's full-page black and white illustrations are of deities and heroes.   6 +

337.   Starbuck, Edwin Diller, ed.   *Familiar Haunts*.   New York: The Macmillan Company, 1930.

This anthology contains "The Golden Touch" and "The Miraculous Pitcher" (Baucis and Philemon) from *A Wonder Book* by Nathaniel Hawthorne (see above).

338.   Stephanides, Menelaos. *Stephanides Brothers' Greek Mythology*. 14
         vols. completed. Translated by Bruce Walter. Illustrated by Yannis
         Stephanides. Athens: Sigma Publications, 1986-.

This collection of picture books encompasses a great many of the
characters and events which constitute ancient Greek mythology. It is
divided into three parts--Series A: The Gods of Olympus, Series B:
Gods and Heroes, and Series C: Heroes. Each volume focuses on one
or two major characters, whose stories are told as completely as
possible. Bits and pieces taken from various ancient Greek sources
(not mentioned in the text) are thoroughly blended into one coherent
narrative. Moreover, in each volume, there are references to stories
in other volumes of the work. Each volume is consistent with the
others in tone, style, and methodology. Sometimes Stephanides uses
the modern Greek names of characters; for example, Hebe is called Ivi.
An index of all names (with pronunciation indicated) in the series may
be found in volumes 13 and 14. The other volumes contain partial
lists. For the young reader, Stephanides adds explanations of ancient
Greek social practices, such as the exposing of infants. In a few
places, he, perhaps to bowdlerize, changes a traditional plot line.
Three examples will suffice: 1) Apollo must serve as the slave of
Admetus because he has killed Python (not because he has killed the
Cyclopes as Euripides states in the *Alcestis*); 2) Daedalus' nephew
accidentally falls off the roof of Athena's temple rather than being
pushed off by his uncle, and 3) Zeus absorbs rather than swallows
Metis.

On every page of every volume striking illustrations in strong colors
attract the young reader's attention and entice him or her into reading
the text, which is in fairly large, bold print. Very brief marginal
annotations serve both to summarize and to aid in locating a specific
passage.

In the epilogue of volume 1 (repeated in several other volumes),
Stephanides states that he has chosen myths which portray "moral
values which hold good the world over" (p. 37). He is fond of
moralizing and/or interpreting. For example, after describing the
goddess Athena going to war for defense of right, he notes, "It is
always the same: when the need arises, the first to throw themselves
into battle are those who love peace most!" (vol. 6, p. 7). Concerning
the death of her children as a punishment for Niobe's pride,
Stephanides comments, "Why are the gods so often unjust to mortals?
Niobe may have been at fault, but she was punished so harshly and
inhumanly that whatever crime she was guilty of pales before the

vengeance that was wreaked on her. The sentence passed on Niobe becomes a condemnation of the gods themselves" (vol. 12, p. 23).

In the epilogue of volume 11, after praising the presentation of moral values in works by Homer and the Greek playwrights, Stephanides states, "we do not accept that the so-called mythology of Apollodorus, written in the 2nd century A.D., is a faithful representation of ancient Greek myth . . . these myths reflect the age in which they were written--an age of rapid decline and corruption" (p. 34). Nevertheless, Stephanides often follows Apollodorus rather than an earlier writer. His account of the events leading up to the castration of Uranus is much closer to Apollodorus' version than to Hesiod's. Stephanides fills in descriptive and narrative details which he finds lacking in the ancient works; for example, he says that whenever Zeus would become angry, "his face would become terrible to behold and blinding sparks would flash from his eyes" (vol. 1, pp. 26-27). In addition to relying heavily on Apollodorus, Stephanides frequently uses material from another work of later antiquity, the *Description of Greece* of Pausanias (2nd century A.D.).

Following is a list of the titles in this collection:

Series A

(Vol. 1)	*The Battle of the Titans: Uranus - Cronus - Zeus*
(Vol. 2)	*The Music of the Gods: Hera-Aphrodite*
(Vol. 3)	*Apollo and His Lyre: Apollo - Hermes*
(Vol. 4)	*The Myth of Persephone: Demeter - Artemis*
(Vol. 5)	*The Golden Throne: Hephaestus - Ares*
(Vol. 6)	*Pallas Athena: Poseidon - Hestia*

Series B

(Vol. 7)	*Deucalion's Flood*
(Vol. 8)	*Prometheus*
(Vol. 9)	*Phaëthon*
(Vol. 10)	*Orpheus and Eurydice*
(Vol. 11)	*Daedalus and Icarus*

Series C

(Vol. 12)	*Europa*
(Vol. 13)	*Heracles*
(Vol. 14)	*Theseus - Perseus* 7 +

339.   *Stories of the Classic Myths: Retold from St. Nicholas.* New York: The Century Company, 1909.

Retellings of ancient Greek and Roman myths which appeared in *St. Nicholas Magazine* are collected in this volume, which provides a fine introduction to classical mythology. The book includes hero tales, stories from Ovid, and chapters which treat of the centaurs and Muses (excellent). The last chapter discusses the importance of studying mythology, explains myths as nature allegories, and describes each of the major deities. The selections, by various authors, including Andrew Lang (see above) and James Baldwin (see above), differ in the extent to which they remain faithful to the ancient accounts. Many of illustrations (in black and white) are finely detailed line drawings with captions.   6 +

340.   Storr, Catherine. *Odysseus and the Enchantress.* Illustrated by Mike Codd. Milwaukee: Raintree Publishers, Inc., 1985.

In this book, Storr describes not only Odysseus' visit to the island of Circe but also his encounters with the Sirens and with Scylla and Charybdis. Though Storr follows Homer's account quite closely, she does change minor details; for example, Circe, called a witch-goddess, lives in a palace rather than a cottage. Action-filled colored illustrations take up more room on each page than the text.   4 +

341.   Storr, Catherine. *Theseus and the Minotaur.* Illustrated by Ivan Lapper. Milwaukee: Raintree Children's Books, 1986.

Following rather closely the account of Theseus and the Minotaur in Robert Graves' *The Greek Myths* (an adult book which is a synthesis of all ancient sources), Storr retells the story in short, clear sentences, adding dialogue and elaborating on Theseus' fight with the monster. Storr refers to the Nereids who helped Theseus to recover Minos' ring as mermaids. Daedalus is spelled Daedelus. The illustrations of this

picture book seem to have been inspired by the ancient ruins at Crete
and Athens.   4+

342.   Storr, Catherine. *The Trojan Horse*. Illustrated by Mike Codd.
         Milwaukee: Raintree Children's Books, 1985.

         This little book provides a good introduction to the Trojan War saga.
         It begins with the abduction of Helen and ends with the departure of the
         Greeks from Troy. Storr concentrates on the main characters--Paris,
         Helen, Odysseus, Achilles, and Priam. She retells the story in her own
         words without undue embellishment.   A note lists her sources as
         Homer's *Iliad* and *Odyssey* and Robert Graves' *The Greek Myths* (an
         adult book which is a synthesis of all ancient sources). Vividly colored
         illustrations, which emphasize the emotions and actions of the
         characters, elucidate the text.   4+

343.   Storr, Francis, ed. *Half a Hundred Hero Tales of Ulysses and the Men
         of Old*. Illustrated by Frank C. Papé. New York: Henry Holt and
         Company, 1911.

         In his preface, Storr points out that the Greek myths "have been
         adapted for young readers by Fénelon, by Niebuhr, by Kingsley, by
         Hawthorne, and yet the last word has not been said. Each new editor
         makes his own selection, chooses some new facet, or displays the jewel
         in a new light" (p. iii). Storr continues the tradition, presenting forty
         original retellings and ten selections from Hawthorne's *Tanglewood
         Tales* (see above).   Heroes range from Phaëthon to Protesilaus to
         Romulus. Eight finely detailed, captioned line drawings show scenes
         described in the text. Some authors follow the ancient sources more
         closely than others.

344.   Strong, Joanna (pseudonym of Caroline Horowitz). *Legends Children
         Love*. Illustrated by Hubert Whatley. New York City: Hart Publishing
         Company, 1950.

         More than half of this book is devoted to stories from ancient Greece
         and Rome, including those of Icarus, Pandora, and Regulus. The rest
         of the book consists of Norse and English legends. In some passages,
         Strong follows the ancient accounts so closely that they are
         recognizable even though Strong does not mention her sources.   In
         other passages, Strong changes plot lines. Sometimes, as in the case

of Remus' murder, the alteration is obviously the result of bowdlerization: Strong states that Remus was accidentally killed (p. 52). In Strong's retelling of the myth of Theseus, Periphetes (Corynetes), who lived at Epidaurus, is called Epidaurus. In her preface, addressed to parents, Strong points out that the adventure and charm of the classical legends captivates children. In her text, she employs a style of writing that lends itself to reading aloud. Each story has a full-page black and white illustration highlighted in one color. A sentence from the text serves as the legend for the illustration.   5+

345.   Strong, Joanna (pseudonym of Caroline Horowitz) and Leonard, Tom B. (pseud.). *A Treasury of the World's Great Myths and Legends for Boys and Girls*. Illustrated by Hubert Whatley. New York: Hart Publishing Company, 1951.

Included in this collection of famous stories are twenty ancient Greek myths, ranging from that of the Trojan Horse to that of Arachne to that of Damon and Pythias; fifteen fables of Aesop; and five Roman legends based on Livy. The selections are condensed retellings of accounts found in ancient literature (no sources other than Aesop are mentioned). Each selection is illustrated with a full-page, captioned line drawing. The print is large; the sentences are short and crisp. *Myths and Legends of the Ages* by Marion N. French (see above) is a revised edition of this book.   4+

346.   Suter, Joanne. *World Myths and Legends: Greek and Roman*. Belmont, California: Fearon/Janus, 1992.

This survey of classical mythology is divided into five parts: "In the Beginning" (creation myths), "Mortals and Their Mistakes," "Love Stories," "Heroes and Their Adventures," and "Great Stories from History." The myths are simplified and bowdlerized, often by the omission of whole sections of a story. Sentences are kept brief and vocabulary basic. Phineus is spelled Phineas. Since Suter generally gives the most famous version of a mythological incident, the classicist will recognize her ancient sources even though she does not cite them. A brief note under the title of each chapter reveals its content and theme. The questions at the end of a chapter review important ideas presented therein. Other features of the book include an introductory chapter on the role of myth, a table of the Greek and Roman deities, and a pronunciation guide. Line drawings, with short legends, draw attention to important scenes. One inconsistency was noted: on p. 5,

Atlas holds up the world; on p. 45, he, as in the ancient works, holds up the sky. This book is part of the World Myths and Legends series.   5+

347.   Swinburne, Laurence and Swinburne, Irene. *Ancient Myths: The First Science Fiction*. Milwaukee: Raintree Children's Books, 1977.

In their introduction, the authors ask their readers to consider which "bionic" hero each of the ancient heroes resembles. Then they relate the stories of Heracles and the Hydra, Perseus and Medusa, Orpheus and Eurydice, and Achilles and Patroclus. Finally, they reveal the modern heroes whom they had in mind. The Swinburnes retell the myths somewhat freely, employing short, uncluttered sentences and modern-sounding dialogue. The only major departure from the ancient accounts is that the Graeae are called witches. Half-page, captioned illustrations, some in color, are scattered throughout the text. Geometric borders around the chapter title and large, dark print make the book even more visually attractive.   4+

348.   Tappan, Eva March, ed. *Myths from Many Lands*. Vol. II of *The Children's Hour*. New York: Houghton, Mifflin and Company, 1907.

This anthology of myth includes seven selections from the corpus of Nathaniel Hawthorne (see above) and five from that of Josephine Preston Peabody (see above). It also contains Scandinavian, Japanese, Slavic, and Indian myths. In her preface, addressed to children, Tappan explains how myths originated. Five photograph-like illustrations (with captions) decorate the classics section of the book while the colored frontispiece shows Pandora.   6+

349.   Tappan, Eva March, ed. *Stories from the Classics*. Vol. III of *The Children's Hour*. New York: Houghton, Mifflin and Company 1907.

A fine introduction to classical literature, this is an anthology of selections from translations and retellings of stories drawn from Herodotus and Livy as well as from Homer, Vergil, and Ovid. In her preface, addressed to children, Tappan presents biographical and stylistic information about each of the ancient authors. Borders around the black and white captioned illustrations make them look like photographs in an album; the colored frontispiece shows Odysseus and Argus. The 1929 edition has colored illustrations throughout.   6+

350.   Thomson, Peggy. *The King Has Horse's Ears*. Illustrated by David
        Small. New York: Simon and Schuster, 1988.

        This story is an adaption of Ovid's version of King Midas and his ass'
        ears.   Only his barber, who has been threatened with death if he
        reveals the secret, knows that King Horace has horse's ears.   He
        whispers the secret into a pond where reeds are growing. A piper uses
        one of these reeds for his pipe. When he plays at the King's wedding,
        the pipe sings out the secret. The barber is saved since the new queen
        decides that she likes her husband's ears. Clip-on horse ears become
        popular, and the barber's business increases. Except for the word
        "retold by" before the author's name, no mention is made of the
        ancient myth. Colorful, caricature-like illustrations feature neoclassical
        furniture and clothing.   4 +

351.   Tomaino, Sarah F. *Persephone: Bringer of Spring*. Illustrated by Ati
        Forberg. New York: Thomas J. Crowell Company, 1971.

        Throughout this book, deep-toned, double-page colored illustrations are
        alternated   with   double-page   black   and   white   illustrations.
        Superimposed is the text, which tells the story of Demeter and
        Persephone in simple language and relatively short sentences. Tomaino
        blends material from the *Homeric Hymn to Demeter* and from Ovid's
        Metamorphoses.   She adds some details; for example, Celeus' role is
        enlarged, and changes others; for example, Persephone eats four
        pomegranate seeds.   4 +

352.   Turska, Krystyna. *Pegasus*. Illustrated by Krystyna Turska.   New
        York: Franklin Watts, Inc., 1970.

        With an abundance of descriptive detail lacking in the material from
        ancient sources on which she bases her account, Turska describes the
        birth of Pegasus, his adventures with Bellerophon, and his function on
        Mount Olympus. Turska also tells the story of Bellerophon, supplying
        psychological insights into the hero.   Turska's large, deep-hued
        illustrations nearly overpower the text.   4 +

353.   Untermeyer, Bryna and Untermeyer, Louis, ed. *Legendary Animals*.
         Vol. 9 of the Golden Treasury of Children's Literature. New York:
         Golden Press, Inc., 1954.

         The chapter on Theseus and the Minotaur in this anthology is a
         condensed and simplified version of Charles Kingsley's retelling in *The
         Heroes; or Greek Fairy Tales for My Children* (see above). Also
         included are the legend of Androcles and the lion and several fables of
         Aesop.   6 +

354.   Untermeyer, Louis. *The Firebringer and Other Great Stories: Fifty-five
         Legends That Live Forever*. Illustrated by Mae Gerhard. New York:
         M. Evans and Company, Inc., 1968.

         Twenty-five legends in this large collection are of particular interest to
         classicists. Stories about Socrates and Julius Caesar are included with
         stories about mythological figures such as Endymion, Atalanta, and
         Pyramus. Several stories explain the derivation of English words, for
         example, *laconic*. In his preface, Untermeyer relates that he has added
         new details and dialogue and has retold the stories in the language of
         his own day. He condenses greatly but always preserves the plot line
         though not the tone of the ancient work. Action-filled line drawings,
         highlighted in green or orange, show scenes described in the text. This
         book was first published in 1964 under the title *The World's Greatest
         Stories: Fifty-five Legends That Live Forever*. It was republished under
         the same title in 1986.   6 +

355.   Untermeyer, Louis. *The World's Great Stories: Fifty-five Legends that
         Live Forever*. Illustrated by Mae Gerhard. New York: M. Evans and
         Company, Inc., 1964 (see preceding entry).

356.   Usher, Kerry. *Heroes, Gods, and Emperors from Roman Mythology*.
         Illustrated by John Sibbick. Vancouver: Schocken Books, 1983.

         Usher presents a survey of Roman history, which serves as the
         framework of the book, as well as retellings of the major myths and
         legends of Rome. The five chapters which are devoted to Roman
         religion discuss beliefs, deities, and rituals. The book contains a
         condensed version of the *Aeneid*, retellings of famous legends from the
         first decade of Livy, the transformation tales of Picus and of the Sibyl,
         and Roman myths about Hercules and Aesculapius. Taking care to

retain important details, the author condenses and paraphrases material from ancient sources (which he mentions).   Features of the book include 18 full-color paintings, 46 black line drawings, an explanation of Roman symbols, and index, and a map.   6+

357.   VanDuyn Southworth, Gertrude (see Southworth, Gertrude VanDuyn).

358.   Vautier, Ghislaine. *The Shining Stars: Greek Legends of the Zodiac*. Adapted by Kenneth McLeish. Illustrated by Jacqueline Bezençon. Cambridge: Cambridge University Press, 1981.

This book is divided into four parts: 1) thumbnail sketches of the main characters in the book, 2) stories about each of the signs of the zodiac, 3) star maps of the zodiacal constellations, and 4) a brief explanation of stars and constellations. The author exercises much poetic license in relating the zodiacal myths. Some of the identifications she makes differ from those in the works of Hyginus and Manilius. Deep-toned borders around lightly tinted pages with copious illustrations make the book especially attractive.   6+

359.   Vautier, Ghislaine. *The Way of the Stars: Greek Legends of the Constellations*.   Adapted by Kenneth McLeish.   Illustrated by Jacqueline Bezençon. Cambridge: Cambridge University Press, 1982.

The maxim "pictures speak louder than words" applies especially well to this book about the constellations. The many illustrations, done in water-color tints and set on pastel pages with deep-toned borders, invite long study. A star map is placed next to each illustration of a constellation. The zodiacal myths are told very freely. There are some inaccuracies; for example, Perseus rather than Bellerophon rides on Pegasus and Jason is from Pherae rather than Iolcus. The book contains directions for making a star-show, star maps of the world, and some astronomical information.   4+

360.   Warren, Robert Penn. *The Gods of Mount Olympus*. New York: Random House, Inc., 1954.

This book serves as a fine starting place for the study of classical mythology. In addition to chapters on each of the major Olympian deities, there are chapters on creation and on the Titanomachy. Warren enumerates the major characteristics and functions of each deity, points out objects associated with each, and relates at least one myth about each. He sometimes discusses the symbolism of a myth. Warren generally gives the most well-known version of a myth; but in the case of Dionysus, he follows Apollodorus' eclectic account. At the beginning of the book, there is a list of the principal deities of classical mythology and a map. The blue highlighting used in the map, in the chapter headings, and in the illustrations makes the book attractive to the eye.   4 +

361.   Watson, Jane Werner, ed. *The Iliad and the Odyssey*. Illustrated by Alice and Martin Provensen. New York: Simon and Schuster, 1956.

This condensation of the *Iliad* and the *Odyssey* includes the highlights of each epic and preserves the tone and even much of the wording of the original works. The first two chapters introduce the young reader to the world of minstrels, to Homer, and to the major characters. The eye-catching colored illustrations, of which there are many throughout the book, greatly aid understanding. This book is a Giant Golden Book.   6 +

362.   Webb, Vivian and Amery, Heather. *The Amazing Adventures of Ulysses*. Illustrated by Stephen Cartwright. Tulsa: Hayes Books, 1981.

Webb and Amery relate in chronological order most of the important incidents recounted by Homer in the *Odyssey*. They begin with the events leading to the Trojan War and end with the secret of the marriage bed. Of Ulysses' travels, only the encounters with the Cyclops, Circe, and Scylla and Charybdis are discussed at length. Through Webb and Amery tend to follow Homer scrupulously, occasionally they change details; for example, Circe lives in a palace rather than a cottage. The last page of the book introduces the reader to Homer and the *Odyssey* and gives a bit of background information. The book has a unique format. The text on every page is divided into small blocks, each of which is accompanied by a whimsical colored illustration.   4 +

363.   Weil, Lisl. *King Midas' Secret and Other Follies*. Illustrated by Lisl
        Weil. New York: McGraw-Hill Book Company, 1969.

        Weil makes the stories of Midas (and his ass' ears), Narcissus, Icarus,
        and the Sphinx into fables. She states the moral at the end of each
        selection, for example, "Don't you make the same mistake!/Narcissus
        fell into a pond,/you may fall into a lake." Weil inserts modern
        details: Midas serves ice cream at his parties; Apollo is Headmaster of
        the Mount Parnassus School of the Arts. Weil arbitrarily changes plot
        lines: Daedalus saves Icarus from drowning, but Narcissus drowns.
        Comical line drawings, highlighted in blue, purple, and yellow,
        complement the text.   4+

364.   Weil, Lisl. *Pandora's Box*. Illustrated by Lisl Weil. New York:
        Atheneum, 1986.

        Weil makes her retelling of Pandora's story unique by changing details
        of Hesiod's account: 1) Pandora is made to teach the human race that
        good things are gifts from the gods, for which they ought to be more
        appreciative; 2) Pandora has a gold box not a jar; and 3) when Pandora
        and Epimetheus open the box to see what is left after the evils have
        flown out, a scented flower rises out of the box, which Epimetheus
        says shows both that there is hope and that good always accompanies
        bad. The light-hearted illustrations are line drawings highlighted in
        shades of brown. The text is printed in brown, too.   4+

365.   West, Michael Philip. *Stories of the Greek Heroes*. Illustrated by J.
        C. B. Knight. London: Longman Group, Ltd., 1955.

        This little book with proportionately small illustrations has a large
        amount of text in fairly large print. In short sentences, West retells the
        stories of Perseus, Theseus, Baucis, Orpheus, Cyclops (Polyphemus),
        and Atalanta. He changes a few significant details. In the ancient
        works, Andromeda must be offered to a sea monster because of a boast
        which her mother has made. In West's version, Andromeda's father
        utters the boast. Ovid relates that Baucis and Philemon were hesitant
        to kill their goose. West says that they were reluctant to kill their hen.
        Orpheus plays a harp rather than a lyre. To aid his young reader,
        West places the definitions of difficult words in parentheses
        immediately after the words. He keeps the number of proper nouns at
        a minimum; for example, Cerberus is called the Dog. West spells
        Eurydice with an *i* rather than a *y* (Euridice). In the prefatory note to

this New Method supplementary reader, West states that he generally employs words within the vocabulary of Books 1 and 2 of the *New Method Readers* and in the vocabulary of the primer of *New Method English for the Arab World*. Extra words are listed at the back of the book, where there are also study questions for each story and a pronunciation guide. Some of the illustrations show scenes described in the text; others are illustrations of italicized words in the text, for example, *passages*. Only the cover illustration is in color.   3 +

366.   Wheeler, Benjamin Ide, ed. *Heroes of Myth and Legend*. Illustrated by Beatrice Stevens. New York: P. F. Collier and Son, 1903.

Wheeler's anthology of hero myths includes the stories of Perseus, Bellerophon, Jason, Odysseus, and Horatius. The substantial selections are derived from Kingsley (see above), Hawthorne (see above), Lamb (see above), and Macaulay (*Lays of Ancient Rome*, 1842).   The delicately colored frontispiece showing Jason is the only illustration of a hero from classical mythology. Wheeler advocates reading to and then with one's child. He believes that myths are especially appealing to children because children prefer to think of inanimate objects, plants, and animals in anthropomorphic terms (p.iii) and because children enjoy exercising their "fathomless credulity" (p. v).   6 +

367.   White, Anne Terry. *The Golden Treasury of Myths and Legends*. Illustrated by Alice and Martin Provensen. New York: Golden Press, 1959.

About half of this Giant Golden Book is devoted to classical mythology. After introductory remarks on the nature of ancient Greek deities and the difference between myth and legend, White retells in a lively but succinct manner the myths of Prometheus, Jason, Hercules, and Oedipus.   She also includes many myths from Ovid.   Though the closeness of White's text to the primary sources varies from passage to passage, White never changes the original story line.   Colorful, eye-catching illustrations are well coordinated with the text.   4 +

368.   White, Anne Terry. *Odysseus Comes Home from the Sea*. Illustrated by Arthur Shilstone. New York: Thomas Y. Crowell, 1968.

Two-thirds of this retelling of the *Odyssey* concerns the events which occurred after Odysseus was conveyed to Ithaca by the Phaeacians.

The only significant omission is the Argus incident. The stories of Odysseus' feigning madness and of the Trojan Horse are woven into the first chapter. Despite having to condense much, White stays close to Homer in tone and wording. Action-filled line drawings show scenes described in the accompanying text. The glossary at the end of the book includes a pronunciation guide. A double-page map shows "Where Odysseus Wandered." 8+

369.   Williams-Ellis, Amabel. *Round the World Fairy Tales*. Illustrated by William Stobbs. New York: Frederick Warne and Co., Inc., 1963.

Included in this collection of international tales is the myth of Odysseus and Circe. In a note at the end of the book, the author 1) discusses the methodology which she employs in retelling stories and 2) gives her sources (she used the Penguin and Loeb translations of the *Odyssey*). Basically, Williams-Ellis condenses and simplifies the ancient account. There are two illustrations (one in color) that show Circe. 4+

370.   Williams, Jay. *Medusa's Head*. Illustrated by Steele Savage. New York: Random House, 1960.

Williams substantially augments the material about Perseus found in the ancient sources with descriptive and narrative passages as well as with dialogue. For example, he begins *in medias res* with Perseus consulting the oracle at Delphi about the whereabouts of the Gorgons--an incident not mentioned in any ancient source. In his account of the marriage of Perseus and Andromeda, Williams follows Hyginus rather than Ovid and Apollodorus. The beige and black illustrations are highlighted in the same blue green color used for the chapter headings. Under each illustration is a sentence caption based directly on the text. 6+

371.   Williamson, Julia, ed. *The Stars Through Magic Casements*. Illustrated by Edna M. Reindel. New York: D. Appleton and Company, 1930.

Williamson offers a collection of stories and poems about constellations, the majority of which are drawn from ancient Greek and Roman mythology. The book includes selections from Robert Frost, Nathaniel Hawthorne (see Hawthorne, *A Wonder Book*), and Henry Wadsworth Longfellow. The chapters written by Williamson follow the ancient sources somewhat closely while some other chapters contain more elaboration. Star maps with imposed figures and line drawings aid understanding, as does the legend under each. The author includes some scientific information along with the mythological explanations about the constellations. In her preface, she discusses the origin of star myths. 6 +

372.   Wilson, Romer (pseudonym), ed. *Green Magic: A Collection of the World's Best Fairy Tales from All Countries.* Illustrated by Violet Brunton. New York: Harcourt, Brace, and Company, 1928.

"Perseus," taken from Kingsley's *The Heroes* (see above), is the only selection from classical mythology in this anthology of tales from around the world. Two full-page line drawings show Danaë. Both are captioned--one incorrectly since it reads "Danaë and the Son of Apollo" instead of "Danaë and the Son of Zeus" (p. 327). In London this book was published by Cape.

373.   Winwar, Frances (pseudonym). *Cupid, The God of Love.* Illustrated by Eleanor Mill. New York: Random House, Inc., 1959.

In this retelling of the myth of Cupid and Psyche, Winwar follows Apuleius (not mentioned in the book) quite closely. She simplifies and adds brisk dialogue. In the first chapter, she includes the stories of Venus' rising from the sea, her being awarded the golden apple, her marriage to Vulcan, and her affair with Mars (Winwar bowdlerizes, stating that Mars and Venus were secretly married), which resulted in the birth of Cupid. Each chapter contains several captioned illustrations. They consist of line drawings shaded in blue. 6 +

374.   Wise, William. *Monster Myths of Ancient Greece.* Illustrated by Jerry Pinkney. New York: G. P. Putnam's Sons, 1981.

Though its title emphasizes monsters, this book is, in reality, an introduction to the Greek heroes Perseus, Bellerophon, Theseus, Hercules, and Odysseus and to the heroine Atalanta. The author tells their stories in short straightforward sentences. He follows the ancient sources, adding details only to increase understanding. The first chapter is a general introduction to ancient Greek culture and mythology. The finely detailed drawings in this large-print book attract attention because they feature brown rather than black ink. The background of the title page is a map of the ancient Greek world.   4+

375.   Witting, Alisoun. *A Treasury of Greek Mythology.* Illustrated by James Barry. Irving-on-Hudson, New York: Harvey House, Inc., 1965.

Witting begins with stories from Ovid's *Metamorphoses* (interrupted by a chapter on Homer), then presents descriptions of important deities, next offers stories about Theseus and Dionysus. Her final chapter consists of suggestions for further reading in classical mythology, with commentary on the books mentioned. In her retellings of the myths, Witting follows her ancient sources carefully. Each introduction to a deity contains both information and interpretative material. Each is accompanied by a full-page illustration of the deity that shows something with which he or she is associated. All the illustrations in the book draw attention because of their distinctive black, orange, and white color scheme. The book has an index (with pronunciation guide) and is available in paperback.   6+

376.   Yolen, Jane. *Wings.* Illustrated by Dennis Nolan. San Diego: Harcourt Brace Jovanovich, Publishers, 1991.

The story of Daedalus is used to show that the ancient Greek gods never failed to punish a man who was proud and clever but not always kind. To achieve her objective, the author, at the end of each page of text, places a line describing the reaction of the deities to the action discussed in the text, for example, "The gods heard his curses and they grew angry." In addition, many of the illustrations (very large and in water colors) have inset illustrations that convey pictorially the reactions of the deities. In an introductory note, Yolen summarizes the information about Daedalus given in ancient sources, names the main sources, and explains *hubris.* The pages of the book lack numbers.   6+

377.   Yonge, Charlotte M. *Young Folks' History of Greece.* Cincinnati: Hitchcock and Walden, 1878.

The first quarter of this child's history of Greece is devoted to classical mythology, which the author believes is "absolutely necessary to the understanding of . . . history and of art" (p. vi). Yonge presents a mythological history of the world from creation to the return of Odysseus from the Trojan War. She points out the time relationship between events in classical mythology and Biblical events. She uses the Latin names of the Olympians. In the process of condensing, Yonge sometimes conflates stories, for example, that of the Titans and that of the Giants. Though most of what she says is substantiated by ancient sources, there are a few inaccuracies; for example, Ate is identified with Eris. Line drawings, some captioned, are scattered throughout the text.   6+

378.   Zaidenberg, Arthur. *How to Draw Prehistoric and Mythical Animals*. Illustrated by Arthur Zaidenberg. London: Abelard-Schuman, Limited, 1967.

The creatures from ancient Greek and Roman mythology which are included in this book are the Centaurs, the Naxian Sphinx, the Chimaera (which also serves as the cover illustration), and three signs of the zodiac--Sagittarius, Aries, and Taurus. In his introduction, Zaidenberg, after telling the young artist-reader that throughout the ages, each artist, using imagination, has added his/her own personal touch to portraits of mythical animals, encourages the budding artist to do the same. In the following two chapters, Zaidenberg discusses materials required and basic shapes and forms that appear in his sketched models of the mythical animals and other creatures which make up the rest of the book.   6+

379.   Zeff, Claudia. *The Amazing Adventures of Hercules*. Illustrated by Stephen Cartwright. London: Usborne Publishing, Ltd., 1982.

Alternating small blocks of text with small blocks of light-hearted illustrative drawings (in color), Zeff tells the story of Hercules, concentrating on his twelve labors. She mentions Hera's enmity and Hercules' slaying of Megera (*sic*) and his sons. She follows the tradition that the labors were undertaken to expiate these murders. In presenting the labors, Zeff adds much descriptive detail. At the end of the book, she notes that Hercules is Heracles' Roman name and comments briefly on Hera, Tiryns, Zeus, Atlas, and Heracles. This book is an English language reader.   4+

380.   Zeff, Claudia. *The Amazing Adventures of Jason and the Golden Fleece*.   Illustrated by Stephen Cartwright.   London: Usborne Publishing, Ltd., 1982.

Zeff tells the story of Jason from his birth to his return to Iolcus with the Golden Fleece. The parts of the Argonautic voyage on which Zeff focuses are the encounters with Amycus, the Harpies, the Clashing Rocks, and the Stymphalian Birds. More than half of this reader concerns the adventures of Jason and Medea. The last page of the book introduces the reader to the *Argonautica* of Apollonius of Rhodes. Zeff's version differs from Apollonius' as follows: 1) Atalanta is an Argonaut; 2) the sons of Boreas kill rather than chase off the Harpies; 3) Jason drinks a magic potion given to him by Medea; and 4) Jason marries Medea in Iolcus. Throughout Zeff's book, both the text and the eye-catching, deep-toned illustrations are arranged in small blocks.   4 +

381.   Zorn, Steven. *Bulfinch's Mythology Coloring Book*.   Illustrated by Helen I. Driggs. Philadelphia: Running Press, 1989.

This introduction to classical mythology is unique. Each page of text (kept at a minimum) is followed by a full-page relevant drawing for the reader to color. The cover of the book has a velcro closure. At the beginning of the book is a 17" by 22" inch pull-out page with drawings for coloring of mythological characters treated of in the book, including Medusa, the Hydra, the Sphinx, the Chimaera, and the Cyclops. Zorn adapts for children some of the most famous myths in Bulfinch's *Age of Fable* (see above). He simplifies, condenses, and updates the language but remains true to Bulfinch, who, is turn, followed his ancient sources conscientiously. Like Bulfinch, Zorn uses the Latin names of the deities. At the bottom of the first page of every selection, the pronunciation of the names of the characters in the selection is indicated. In his introduction, Zorn familiarizes his young reader with the major deities and comments on Thomas Bulfinch and his works. Zorn's employment of rather difficult vocabulary words may prove daunting to the beginning reader.   3 +

Index to Introductory Material

Numbers are those of pages.

Title Index

Numbers are those of entries in the Annotated Bibliography.

Illustrator Index

Numbers are those of entries in the Annotated Bibliography.

Chronological Index

Numbers are those of entries in the Annotated Bibliography. Many of the books have several editions. Generally, the earliest edition of a book was reviewed. Since the myths are timeless, the age of a book does not necessarily render it obsolete.

97, 98, 112, 116, 129,
138, 139, 142, 143,
150, 164, 200, 201,
267, 310, 344, 345,
353, 360, 361, 365,
367, 373

1960-1969: 4, 48, 54, 59, 64, 71,
73, 75, 89, 94, 95,
96, 126, 130, 131,
132, 133, 135, 136,
137, 140, 141, 144,
145, 146, 167, 169,
175, 183, 184, 185,
186, 195, 198, 205,
206, 229, 238, 245,
261, 263, 266, 268,
289, 291, 309, 312,
313, 317, 318, 319,
321, 326, 332, 354,
355, 363, 368, 369,
370, 375, 378

1970-1979: 3, 12, 15, 16, 32, 52,
61, 74, 78, 90, 91,
101, 102, 103, 117,
118, 119, 120, 121,
122, 123, 124, 125,
128, 168, 172, 173,
194, 209, 212, 213,
215, 221, 225, 226,

227, 228, 230, 240, 243, 244, 252,
274, 275, 276, 277, 278, 279, 287,
288, 290, 292, 293, 307, 315, 320,
329, 347, 351, 352

1980-1989: 19, 20, 56, 66, 72,
82, 83, 84, 85, 86,
87, 88, 92, 93, 108,
109, 113, 127, 134,
154, 163, 165, 170,
171, 176, 177, 180,
181, 190, 210, 214,
216, 217, 218, 234,
235, 237, 239, 247,
248, 249, 250, 251,
255, 256, 257, 258,
259, 260, 284, 295,
296, 297, 298, 299,
300, 301, 302, 303,
304, 305, 306, 311,
328, 338, 340, 341,
342, 350, 356, 358,
359, 362, 364, 374,
379, 380, 381

1990-1992: 70, 80, 106, 107,
155, 166, 178, 231,
241, 242, 285, 324,
330, 331, 346, 376

no date: 22, 79

Mythological Index

Numbers are those of entries in the Annotated Bibliography.

General Index

This index includes authors and works (both ancient and modern) cited in the Annotated Bibliography; general subject headings, such as hero myths; and miscellaneous items, such as the names of artists mentioned. For individual characters and topics, see Mythological Index. Also see Title Index, Illustrator Index, and Chronological Index. The numbers in this index are those of the entries in the Annotated Bibliography.

About the Compilers

ANTOINETTE BRAZOUSKI is an instructor in the Department of Foreign Languages and Literature at Northern Illinois University. An authority on Augustan literature, classical mythology, and classical epic poetry, her publications have appeared in *Helios*, *The Classical Bulletin*, and *The Ancient History Bulletin*.

MARY J. KLATT is Mediated Search Services Coordinator and Information Services Librarian at the library of Loyola University of Chicago Medical Center.